PRACTICAL

SILVER-SMITHING

&

JEWELRY

PRACTICAL

SILVER-SMITHING

&

JEWELRY

KEITH SMITH

VAN NOSTRAND REINHOLD COMPANY

NEW YORK CINCINNATI TORONTO LONDON MELBOURNE

Acknowledgements

I would like to thank the British Steel Corporation for giving me permission to publish their photographs of stainless steel jewelry, and Miss Susan Hare, Librarian of Goldsmiths' College, London, for her help with the remaining photographs. Thanks also to all the designers whose work is reproduced and to the editorial staff of Studio Vista for their help and encouragement. The stainless steel jewelry (Figs 87, 90, 93 and 94) was designed and made at Loughborough College of Art.

Published in 1975 by Van Nostrand Reinhold Company
A Division of Litton Educational Publishing Inc.
450 West 33rd Street
New York, NY 10001

16 15 14 13 12 11 10 9 8 7 6 5 4 3 2 1

Library of Congress Cataloging in Publication Data
Smith, Keith, 1929-
    Practical silver-smithing and jewelry.

    Bibliography: p.
    Includes index.
    1. Silversmithing. 2. Jewelry making. I. Title. II. Title: Silver-smithing and jewelry.
TS730.S46   1975   739.27   75-9988

ISBN 0-442-27791-1

Contents

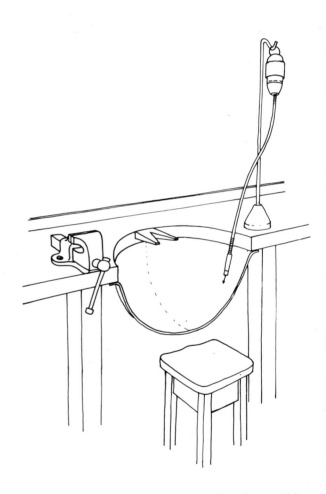

Fig. 1   Typical silversmithing
and jewelry bench

6

1 The Workshop

As you work through this book you will discover what sort of tools you need to practise each different technique. However, I will start by making some general recommendations about common tools, your workshop and the quality and organization of your equipment.

The ideal workshop is equipped with sturdy benches with tops made from beech at least 50 mm (2 in.) thick. The legs may be of softwood 65×95 mm (2·5×3·75 in.) and should be rigidly braced so that the whole structure can endure heavy hammering and the strains of heaving on vice handles. Traditional benches have a semicircular cut-out at which you sit and work. This cut-out allows you to arrange your tools around you and to catch filings and clippings of valuable metal in a leather or plastic apron which is nailed to the underside of the bench. Alternatively you can have a wood or metal tray in which to catch scrap, and some people prefer this arrangement because they can deposit small tools on it as they work.

In the centre of the semicircular cut-out there should be a hardwood bench pin and this is an absolutely essential part of the silversmith's and jeweller's equipment. It should project 100 mm (3·9 in.) from the bench and be 80 mm (3·15 in.) wide and 30 mm (1·18 in.) thick. It should have a V cut out of it so that two prongs with flat ends project towards you, and it should be tapered on one face so that each prong has a thin edge at its extremity. The pin should have a full-width tongue, 15 mm (0·59 in.) thick which fits a slot in the bench 15 mm (0·59 in.) below the top surface. The tongue should project from the lower half of the pin so that the flat surfaces of the bench pin and of the bench top are flush. However, if the bench pin is turned over, the sloping surface of its tapered face will be set 15 mm (0·59 in.) below the bench top. In this position the pin can be used as a rest for work that is being filed or stoned, because not only is the angle comfortable for working, but you can also use the edge of the bench above the pin as a stop against which to hold work steady. When the flat face is uppermost and flush with the bench, it is easy to use a piercing saw. The bench pin is expendable and can have grooves and slots cut and filed in its surface and edges to enable work to be held and fashioned efficiently.

You should have a vice on one side of your work point; on the left-hand side if you are right-handed, and on the right-hand side if you are left-handed. This allows you to turn easily and use any tool held in the vice. The vice should be situated over a bench leg so that heavy hammering is absorbed, and if you are a silversmith it should be a large engineers' vice and must be bolted down. If you are a jeweller something much smaller may suit you, and it might even be secured to the bench with a screw clamp.

The vice will require some detachable, soft jaw covers to hold soft or highly finished work without damaging it. Aluminium angle section or bought plastic jaws are ideal. All vice accessories like this must be constantly re-surfaced and inspected to make sure that no hard and sharp fragments are embedded in their working surfaces.

If you are a home worker you will be lucky to possess a heavy bench, or even a workshop, but if you are a jeweller you can work on the kitchen table. A piece of board can be placed over the table and a bench pin held in place with a G-cramp, which will also secure the board to the table. You can clamp a vice in position in a similar manner.

You will, of course, need a stool or chair to sit on, and you may prefer a revolving seat so that you can vary the height and turn easily from bench pin to vice.

Facilities for heating metal are, of course, essential for all silversmiths and jewellers, and the ideal workshop for a silversmith will have a revolving hearth on an asbestos covered bench. The hearth should have one or two large fire bricks in it with ribbed surfaces, or with a coarse iron mesh resting on top of them (fig. 2). In addition you should always have a heap of broken pieces of brick for propping work at a suitable working angle. Some people prefer clinker in their hearths, but it is perilously easy to drop a small but important component into it, and to lose it for ever. If you are a jeweller you can anneal or solder your work at your work point on a piece of asbestos, a fire brick or a refractory brick for a kiln. A small turntable will allow you to solder much more conveniently.

Fig. 2 Revolving hearth with ribbed fire brick and coarse wire mesh

A silversmith's hearth should have a large canopy over it with an extractor fan to draw away fumes, and the whole area should be screened from bright light and painted matt black so that you can see the colour of your metal as you heat it.

The gas supply for heating metal can be piped in from the mains, if mains gas is available, or supplied in bottles. A piped gas supply is usually used in conjunction with an air supply which is mixed with the gas in the torch to make a hotter flame. The air may be supplied from a compressor, occasionally from an oxygen bottle, or blown in by the mouth for a jewelry torch. Compressors or blowers can be bought at varying costs and in a variety of sizes from an air tools firm or any machine tool warehouse. Most silversmiths will agree that mains gas used with compressed or blown air produces a more versatile and sensitive flame than a bottle gas torch. Air is usually mixed with a bottle gas flame being drawn through holes in the head of the torch as the gas burns and the resultant flame is very hot but not very large. A mains gas torch of the best sort has two taps, one controlling the flow of gas and one controlling the air quantity; various combinations of settings on these taps can give a wide variety of flame sizes. A large flame without too much air will envelop a large piece of work to build up heat quickly, while a flame with less gas and more air will provide a more intense local flame around a solder joint.

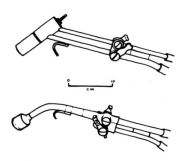

Fig. 3 Mains gas supply torches with separate gas and air control taps

A bottle gas flame takes longer to build up the initial heat, and may have a flame too large for easy soldering. However the choice of torch must be a matter for individual preference.

This choice is far less critical for jewellers, many of whom prefer bottle

Fig. 4 (above) Mains gas jewelry torch with separate taps for gas and air

(below) Mains gas jewelry torch with air supplied through a mouth pipe

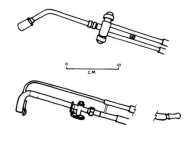

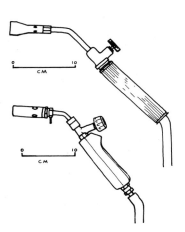

Fig. 5 Bottle gas jewelry torches

gas. Mains torches for jewellers are available from several manufacturers and you should select one with gas and air controls (fig. 4). If you work at home you will almost certainly choose bottle gas because it is portable and can be used for all sorts of do-it-yourself tasks. In selecting a bottle gas torch (fig. 5) choose one which can be connected to the bottle with a hose, because integral torch and bottle outfits tend to flare when the bottle is tilted to divert the flame downwards. Bottle gas should only be used as recommended by the manufacturers, and makeshift connections and non-standard hosing must never be used. You can also buy interchangeable nozzles for bottle gas torches so that varied flame sizes can be easily achieved. This is a point that you should check before buying your torch. Check also that the gas tap on the torch is easy and painless to turn and hold. If you want to be well equipped, a double outlet on the gas bottle will enable you to have two torches of different sizes for instant use.

The selection of a suitable mains gas torch is difficult because it is not easy to obtain impartial advice or a demonstration, but in Britain you should contact your local Gas Board or the Technical Advisory Committee of the Worshipful Company of Goldsmiths who have issued an excellent booklet on the subject.

A comparatively new development in soldering fine jewelry, especially gold work, is the microflame gas generator. This is a piece of equipment that produces oxy-hydrogen gas from distilled water. The gas is passed through methyl-ethyl ketone to render it more volatile, after which it is burnt in a miniature torch. The flame is very hot and concentrated, making it most suitable for intricate wire work. The torch has several nozzles so that a variety of flame sizes can be achieved. The equipment is not cheap, but can prove invaluable to a professional jeweller. The manufacturers' instructions must be adhered to most strictly.

Metal that has been heated needs cooling, washing, and cleaning in a suitable pickle. In a well equipped workshop an acid or pickle tank will be situated, with the sink, next to the hearth, and it will share the same canopy so that fumes can be drawn away. The tank should be made of lead backed with iron or steel to add strength, and it should be heated so that the cleansing can be effected as quickly and efficiently as possible. The heat can be supplied by a gas burner underneath, or by an immersion heater with a thermostat. The tank can be filled with dilute sulphuric acid or a proprietary brand of safety pickle. Sulphuric acid will work cold, but the safety pickle must be used hot. Sulphuric acid should be diluted with 8-10 parts water. Remember to add the acid to the water. On no account add water to acid because the mixture may erupt and burn you. The safety pickle should be used as suggested by the suppliers. If you work at home you can keep your pickle or acid in a heatproof glass bowl, and if you need to heat it, use a tripod and a spirit lamp. I have warmed pickle sufficiently in a plastic margarine container by floating it in hot water. It goes without saying, of course, that in the home acids and even safety pickles must be kept and used under the most stringent care.

You will need tongs or tweezers for handling hot metal and for putting it in and taking it out of acid. These can be purchased from jewellers' and silversmiths' warehouses, or you can make them from copper, gilding

9

metal, or nickel silver. Iron or steel tongs must never be used in acid.

When your metal is rinsed in the sink, you will need long-handled brushes to scrub it to remove all traces of oxide scale. Brushes with bristles all around the end can be bought for cleaning inside holloware. Jewelry can be cleaned with smaller brushes, and toothbrushes may prove as useful as any. You should keep a box of pumice powder by the sink as an aid to cleansing metal.

Wet metal must be dried before you hammer it on precious stakes. You can keep a box of rags or cotton waste, or a barrel of sawdust by the sink. In a very busy workshop an electric hot-air hand dryer is an excellent investment. Never use the domestic towel; caretakers and housewives become very upset!

The area in which you polish metal needs organizing. In the ideal workshop such a dirty process should be partitioned off from the main working area, but the operator ought to be visible in case of accident. A silversmith needs a powerful polishing motor (fig. 6) which should have twin spindles and revolve at approximately 2,900 r.p.m. It should have ball race bearings and be powerful enough to stand considerable pressure on the polishing mops without slowing or stopping. Polishing motors should be bolted to a very sturdy bench which should have an aluminium covered top which curves up behind and over the top of the motors. The aluminium sheet can terminate under a shelf over the top of the bench and the motors. Safety authorities may insist upon rubber sleeves over the revolving spindles of the motors. An ideal workshop will have an extractor system built into the polishing bench so that fluff, dirt, and valuable metal traces can be collected in a bin. It is possible to improvise and build your own equipment. I have visited two jewellers' workshops in which the cowls for the polishing mops have been made from tin kettles! Cut a segment from the side of the kettle to allow the mop to be used; the handle is, of course, removed; and the spout cut short and joined by a tube to a small vacuum cleaner under the polishing motor, which sucks all the waste into a bag.

A smaller motor can be used by jewellers, but it should still be strong enough for the job. If you work at home you will need a small motor that can be plugged into the domestic electricity supply, and it is possible to buy some models with a flexible drive shaft at one end for delicate grinding and polishing. Many jewellers use an electric motor suspended by their workspace (fig. 7) with a flexible drive shaft for polishing their work. You would normally have this on the right of the bench if you are right-handed.

A large workshop may need a variety of mechanical equipment not already described, and this should all be carefully placed for reasons of convenience and safety. Such equipment might include an engineer's lathe, a spinning lathe, a universal milling machine, a linisher or band facer, a vertical drill, a band saw with as many speeds as possible, and a pantagraph engraving machine. There is, of course, other equipment described elsewhere in the book. Jewellers can equip themselves with miniature versions of some of the equipment, such as lathes and vertical drills.

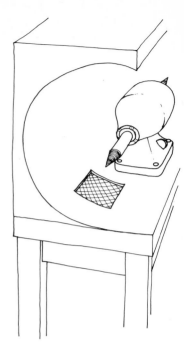

Fig. 6   Polishing bench with polishing motor

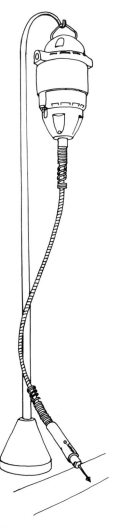

The home worker need not feel that the absence of this equipment is a bar to the production of fine work; ingenuity and careful designing can overcome most problems.

Silversmiths and jewellers require a wide range of hand tools such as files, pliers, hammers and saws and it is a good idea to devise handy racks around the workspace. Files become blunted if they are piled on top of each other, and hammers treated similarly will cover your sheet metal with replicas of all the cuts and bruises that will soon adorn their striking surfaces. Needle files can be kept in holes in wood blocks and so can chasing tools, dental burrs and polishing mops. Large polishing mops will pick up grit if kept on the polishing bench or a shelf and should be hung on a nail board. Ring triblets should be kept in a rack, and stake heads can be kept on shelves with holes for their pegs to fit into. Jewellers' findings, cotter pins and small items of every sort should be organized in nests of drawers.

You should take care over the quality of your tools because good tools, though expensive, will repay with long service. For specialist tools you are advised to go to a specialist supplier rather than the local tool supermarket. You should, for instance, always buy pliers with a box joint rather than a half joint because box joints are not easily strained by the twisting and bending action that the jeweller and silversmith often has to use on wires. You won't often find pliers with a box joint at the average hardware store. There are mail order firms for those who live far from jewelry and silversmithing centres.

Finally, remember to organize your workshop with safety requirements in mind. Don't put your flames by the only door! If you have a large workshop with several people working in it install stop buttons around the walls so that if anyone gets into difficulty it is easy to stop all machinery.

Fig. 7 Suspended pendant polishing and grinding motor

2 Metals

There are many metals that a silversmith or jeweller can use. This chapter aims to discuss each briefly and simply and to give you basic information on their most important characteristics.

Copper

Melting point: 1083°C
Specific gravity: 8·95
Copper is attractive for its colour and for its softness and easy working characteristics. Its very softness, however, is also one of its disadvantages because it is easily damaged during storage or in the course of working, and it is a slow and tedious job to bring it back to a flaw-free surface. It does, however, acquire a fine, soft finish after years of hand-polishing. It is not suitable for casting. It should be annealed by heating to a dull red and quenching in cold water.

Brass (60% copper, 40% zinc)

Melting point: 1015°C
Brass is useful to the silversmith who needs to include turned or machined components in a base metal design. It is quite unsuitable for high temperature silver-soldering because it tends to collapse suddenly. It is also unsuitable for many of the hand processes such as raising and sinking because of its hardness. You cannot use it for box making using silver solders because flat sheets of brass tend to warp easily when heated with a gas torch. You can use it for spinning.

Gilding metal (approximately 90% copper, 10% zinc)

Melting point: above 1000°C
Gilding metal strikes the happy medium between the qualities of brass and copper. It possesses some of the hardness of brass when it has been work hardened, and much of the softness of copper when it has been annealed. At all times it takes a better finish than copper, and, unlike brass, it is reasonably stable under heat and does not collapse or warp unduly. It is the best all-purpose metal for anyone who does not want, or cannot afford, to use silver.

Bronze (approximately 90% copper, 6% tin, 3% zinc, 1% lead)

Melting point: above 1000°C
Specific gravity: 9

Bronze is very hard and some alloys are ideal for machining. For those who have oxygen and propane or oxyacetylene equipment and want to use a hard, non-precious metal for lost wax, centrifugal or vacuum casting, bronze is the ideal metal. It is also possible to cast bronze into cuttlefish. A good scrap merchant or a local engineering factory may sell you suitable scrap.

Nickel silver (nickel, copper and zinc in various proportions)

Nickel silver is a very hard metal. Some people like it for its colour, and it is popular in secondary schools for jewelry, sunk dishes, or cylindrical boxes. It is not suitable for use in large flat areas, such as rectangular boxes because it tends to warp under heat. It is very suitable for spinning and stamping, and has been used extensively for holloware and cutlery in the trade. It is also useful for brooch pins and rivets, and the British Assay Office will allow it to be used with silver brooches, providing, of course, that it is not soldered to the silver. In the United States, the stamping of gold and silver is regulated by law.

Stainless steel (18/8 grade for general use)

Stainless steel represents a considerable challenge to the designer. If it is heated extensively, and to a high temperature, it develops a hard, black oxide on the surface which must be removed with a special pickle, which in turn leaves a dull surface that requires hard work to re-polish it. It is basically harder than all other silversmiths' and jewellers' materials, but it is, nevertheless, easy to damage the surface with careless handling. A damaged stainless steel surface is much harder to repair than any other material. It is possible to solder it with a low-melting-point silver solder and a special flux, but this does not make a strong joint, and a fillet of solder around the joint will be essential to strengthen it. It can be pressed into very shallow forms, bent and folded, sunk into shallow shapes, pierced with good quality saws, and woven and knotted in wire form. It can also be cut with a welding torch to make attractive burnt holes and can be forged at red heat.

Aluminium

Melting point: 659·7°C
Specific gravity: 2·60
Aluminium is usually looked upon as a service material rather than a production material. It is very useful in a silversmiths' workshop because it can be used for prototypes or quick models of difficult ideas. Aluminium can be an excellent spinning medium, and it responds well to sinking, folding, and bending. Secondary schools use aluminium for non-soldered work, and it can be used for cuttlefish casting provided that a large pouring head is cut in the bone so that a little weight will force the molten metal into the mould. Aluminium is also an excellent material from which to make soft vice clamps.

Lead

Melting point: 327·4°C
Specific gravity: 11·40
Lead is a useful service material for the silversmith, but it is also a dangerous one in a practical sense and as a health hazard. It can be used as a mould into which short runs of identical objects can be stamped or pressed. In this case the lead should be kept in large, thick cakes, or in a metal container, and the die should be hammered into the surface to make the mould while the lead is hot, but not, of course, molten. Lead can also be used as a filling material for tubes or spouts which are to be bent or hammered. Objects which are to be bent should be coated inside with whitening. However, lead must not be used or melted on benches and hearths on which precious metals are used because if traces of lead are ground into such metals, or picked up on the hearth, subsequent heating will cause serious holes to be burnt into the surfaces. Lead should be melted only in well ventilated places. You must wash your hands after using it, and children should not be allowed to work it at all.

Silver

Silver is the all-purpose, reasonably priced silversmiths' and jewellers' precious metal. With skill and care, and the right alloy there is nothing that cannot be achieved in silver, such is its ductility and quality. Silver is commonly used in three different alloys.

Standard silver (92·5% pure silver)
Melting point: 890°C
Specific gravity: 10·50
Used for most purposes.

Brittania silver (95·84% pure silver)
Melting point: 920°C
Originally introduced for plate, to prevent craftsmen from clipping the edges of the then standard silver coins to make plate, it is much softer than standard silver and requires some special designing. It can be used for difficult raising or sinking projects.

Enamelling silver
This is a very pure silver to which enamels will adhere firmly. It has a melting point which allows enamels to be heated to a high temperature.

Silver can be obtained in sheet of all thicknesses, wire of many sections, and tube in ring sizes, and several smaller sizes for structural and decorative purposes. Most dealers will cut silver to any shape.

Silver solder

There is a very wide range of silver solder available for all sorts of purposes and for use at many different working temperatures. Solder is available in sheet or in sticks, according to the requirements of the user.

When soldering silver it is essential that solder of the correct purity be used, irrespective of the melting temperature. In Great Britain the solder must contain sufficient silver to satisfy the assay authorities, and anyone using silver is advised to obtain solders from a recognized bullion dealer and to make sure that they are buying assayable solder. Assayable solder is generally available in four grades: enamelling, which melts at 800°C; hard – 775°C; medium – 750°C; and easy – 725°C. This range of solders allows you to carry out several consecutive soldering operations on a piece of work with no risk of melting joints already soldered. Work which is to be enamelled should be soldered only with enamelling solder because most enamels melt at about 800°C. Generally speaking, the lower the melting point of solder, the less controllable it is, and the greater the chance of it running out of a joint and onto a surface where it is not wanted. The craftsman who can learn to restrict solder-melting temperatures to the close proximity of the joints, can complete a job using the same solder in several places, and so avoid using easy solders altogether.

There is also a wide range of silver brazing alloys for joining base metals and the leading bullion dealers will advise you and provide you with data about them and the special fluxes to use with them. These alloys must never be used for soldering silver.

Gold

Gold is available from only a few leading bullion dealers. In Great Britain it is supplied only on production of a licence that is issued by the Bank of England. Licences are issued only to manufacturing or repairing jewellers, or to a college engaged in advanced courses or part-time adult studies. If you wish to qualify for a licence as a designer-craftsman, you must persuade your bullion dealer to issue you with an application form, add to it your qualifications, ask your bank to sign it, and send it to the Bank of England for approval. In the United States, no such licensing is required, and anyone may own gold.

Gold is available in a variety of qualities, usually determined by Assay Office standards on the one hand, and the craftsman's requirements and wealth on the other hand. Wedding rings are usually very pure (22 carat), while all good jewelry is 18 carat. Fourteen carat and 9 carat golds are also used, though the lower the purity the more critical the working characteristics, and with 9 carat gold cracks can appear with age and climatic changes. Gold can be obtained in various colours in all carats. Each alloy has its own characteristics for working and soldering, and the beginner is advised to consult his bullion dealer or to ask for data before rashly spending large sums of money. Gold is available in sheet, wire and tube of all sizes and various sections. Each quality and colour of gold has appropriate solders.

3 Sinking

Sinking is the technique employed in the production of dishes and bowls which are to be of shallow to medium depth and which require thick edges. A chalice is a good example of this kind of bowl.

The technique is suitable for gilding metal, copper and silver but would be tedious and painful with stainless steel – though not impossible. The gauge of metal should be at least 1·62 mm (0·064 in.) but may be thicker according to the depth and the edge thickness demanded by the design. It is necessary to determine the dimensions of the metal sheet from which the vessel is to be made, and in the case of sinking it is always cut to exactly the same size as the plan form of the vessel. After annealing the metal and trimming the edge with a file, mark it out with a series of concentric pencil lines spaced 5 mm (0·2 in.) apart, and starting at the outer edge.

The tools you need for sinking are a hammer with a suitably domed face and a clean steel block which may, if heavy enough, rest on the bench, but should otherwise be held in a vice. The exact choice of hammer depends upon the working requirements. A shallow dish will require only a gentle dome on the hammer, and you can even use a pear-shaped wood mallet. For a deep, well curved form you will need a hammer that reaches in easily and has a well domed face. Hold the metal blank in contact with the steel block and strike it with the hammer on the line 5 mm (0·2 in.) in from the edge (fig. 9). Continue striking, overlapping each hammer blow, and working along the line until you return to your first hammer blow. Now start another row inside the first and overlapping it, and then a third and so on until you reach the centre of the blank, and have hammered the surface completely except for the outer 5 mm (0·2 in.). You will now find that your flat blank has become a shallow dish, though the plan size and edge thickness are unaltered.

This is a suitable moment to consider what has happened to your metal and therefore to understand the technique exactly. The soft metal has been pinched many times between hard hammer and block which has the effect of spreading and thinning it (fig. 10). Because a wide band of metal at the perimeter of the blank is unworked and unaltered the spreading metal cannot be accommodated by an enlargement of the plan and therefore bulges into a dish. Greater depth is achieved by hammering the metal several times, but after each complete hammering the job must be annealed to prevent damage to the metal and discomfort and pain to the hand that holds it! It is very important not to thin the metal too much, especially where a base or handle is to be attached, or the body will collapse in the course of everyday use.

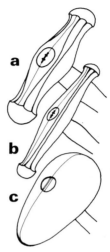

Fig. 8
a Heavy sinking hammer
b Light sinking hammer
c Boxwood sinking mallet

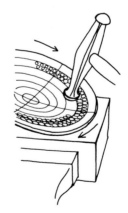

Fig. 9 Sinking a dish on a metal block that is held in a vice

Fig. 10 Section of a piece of metal that has been sunk, showing the edge that has not been hammered on the right

Fig. 11 Sinking a triangular dish in two ways

It is also most important to mark the blank with pencil lines for each course of sinking, to be guided by the lines and to overlap each hammer blow and row of hammer blows if you are to produce quickly a form which is true in all its contours. The direction of hammering must be varied for different plan forms. A round bowl may be worked clockwise by a right-handed craftsman, or anti-clockwise by those who use the left hand, but for a long form, oval or rectangular for instance, these methods are unsuitable because the dish will twist and lose its symmetrical form. In such a case, a course of hammering in a clockwise direction, followed by a course in an anti-clockwise direction should be effective. Alternatively, work from each end to the centre or develop some other method which common sense tells you will neutralize the tendency to twist. In any case you should check the job after each annealing and any twist or inaccuracy should be removed by hand pressure or by pushing the dish against the bench. As the vessel approaches the required form it may be checked with templates to ensure absolute accuracy with the design. Alternatively, take measurements and hold the vessel over the design elevation to check by eye. View it from every conceivable angle to make sure that the form is exactly what you visualized when you drew your design. Remember that in designing you were drawing upon your judgement and experience which are never faultless. In front of you, you now have the design in three dimensions and there is no disgrace in altering it slightly and so continuing the design process throughout the process of production.

As soon as you are satisfied that you have produced the required shape the vessel is ready for planishing (see Chapter 9).

At this point it is worth considering some design opportunities and limitations in relation to the technique of sinking, always remembering that rules and guide lines are open to intelligent 'bending' and abuse and it is indeed through such digressions that a design breakthrough may be achieved. It is interesting to look at the different ways in which a common plan may be worked to produce vessels of different appearances. Fig. 11 shows an equilateral triangular blank which has been sunk to a variety of depths, and by two basic methods. Blank a has been sunk on a concentric triangular basis which has kept the edge on a horizontal plane, but blanks b and c have been sunk to different depths by hammering in a concentric circular basis, and this has the effect of raising the points to give a strong character to the form. It is not difficult to visualize similar movements in square, rectangular, or pear-shaped blanks. In assessing a technique like sinking, eye it hungrily and ask, 'How can I exploit it, what will it do for me?' The manipulation of sheet metal is an exciting business, but don't lose sight of the need to refine your proportions and forms through drawing, modelling, and experimenting.

4 Raising

Raising is the technique which may be employed in the production of holloware of medium to extreme depth from one sheet of metal without any soldered seams.

The technique is suitable for forming copper, gilding metal and silver. The gauge of metal should be at least 0·9 mm (0·036 in.) but many people prefer 1 mm (0·04 in.) or even, exceptionally, 1·2 mm (0·048 in.). You must establish the size of the metal blank needed to produce a specific form, and this can only be done with the aid of an accurate full-size design elevation of the proposed vessel. The traditional silversmith's method of estimating a blank for most shapes is to measure the height of the body and add it to the measurement of the average diameter (fig. 12). The result represents the diameter of the blank. An alternative method is to measure on the design elevation, the diagonal between the centre and the edge of the form. This measurement represents the radius of the metal blank. Neither method is satisfactory on a form which has a broad, flat base and a narrow neck. In such a case it is necessary to add the height to the widest dimension of the elevation to arrive at the diameter of the blank (fig. 13). Each method is an estimate whose accuracy depends on the technique of the craftsman. Some stretch the metal a little, others thicken it, but with experience allowances may be made for individual needs.

The tools required for raising vary according to personal likes and loyalties. In the early stages when the work is being hollowed, a pear-shaped mallet or a large blocking hammer and a sandbag are essential. During raising, you may use metal hammers of various weights. The raising face of each hammer is flat, but has rounded edges and corners to prevent deep and undesirable cuts in the surface of the work (fig. 14). The width of face varies from hammer to hammer. Use narrow faces on small raisings, or where the diameter of the vessel is very narrow. Some craftsmen prefer wood (fig. 15) or horn raising hammers and all employ them at times. If a piece of work has been thinned, recourse to a wood or horn mallet will lessen the risk of further thinning and should allow the metal to thicken again. Wood raising mallets must be constantly re-sharpened if they are to prove really effective.

The metal may be hammered over a variety of stakes. The early hammering is best performed on as solid a stake as possible so that the full effect of the hammer blows may be utilized. Any 'spring' or 'give' in the stake will result in a slower and less effective raising. Important features of the stake include the convex profile of the top surface, the rounded upper corner of the end, and the angle of the end plane, which will allow

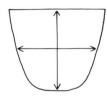

Fig. 12 Finding the diameter of a blank

Fig. 13 Calculating a blank for a wide-bottomed and narrow-necked vessel

Fig. 14 Metal raising hammer

Fig. 15 Boxwood raising mallet

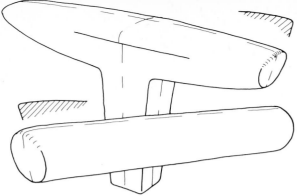

Fig. 16 Raising stake with one wide and one narrow end, and (below) steel bar converted to a raising stake (sections showing profiles of one end)

Fig. 17 Hollowing a blank on a sandbag with a wood mallet prior to raising

Fig. 18 Section to illustrate technique of raising

forms with inward sloping sides and flat bottoms to be raised. Should this type of stake not be available, a round steel bar may be modified and used in a vice. A few craftsmen prefer to undertake early raising on stakes held in a horse. Vibration is a problem here, although this method can be invaluable when, for instance, access through a narrow neck is difficult.

And now to hollowing and raising in detail. Cut your metal to the required size, trim it with a file, using soft jaws if you hold it in a vice, and finally, anneal it. The metal must now be hollowed as follows. Place the blank on a sandbag and strike it in the centre with a pear-shaped mallet or metal blocking hammer (fig. 17). Continue striking, turning the blank with one hand and circling the centre in ever increasing courses until you are close to the edge. At this point finish the hammering on the end-grain of a tree trunk or wood block, smoothing all creases away. Never hammer the edge of the blank on a sandbag because it will lacerate the leather and eventually ruin the sandbag. The inexperienced craftsman may, at this stage, have produced a sadly warped dish shape. The metal should be annealed, trued by pressing it against the bench over the sandbag, or twisting it with the hands, and hollowed again with more concentration upon a true and regular action. The blank should normally be hollowed three times before you begin raising. Too many courses of hollowing will thin the metal, as in sinking, and will result in a structurally unsound body, probably of outsize proportions.

To establish the point at which raising should begin, hold the hollowed work over the design elevation and mark the point at which its form departs from that of the design. Scribe the outer surface of the hollowed work from this point outwards with pencil circles spaced at 5–10 mm (0.2–0.4 in.) intervals, working from an accurate centre. New circles should be scribed befor each new course of raising as an essential aid to producing accurate work.

To begin raising place the work upon the stake, ensuring that the proposed starting point is in contact with the front top corner of the raising stake. Tilt the work so that its edge is about 2 cm (0.75 in.) above the convex surface of the stake. Strike the surface of the work with the raising hammer slightly in front of the point of contact and the soft sheet metal will be hammered downwards onto the surface of the stake (fig. 18). Hold the hammer handle high so that the front edge of the hammer face makes a distinct step on the surface of the work. Drop the hammer handle at your peril, because you will push the metal before you and thin it disastrously. Continue striking, revolving the work and overlapping each hammer blow until you have completed a ridge all around the work. Start striking once again to add a new course of hammer blows, and then another, and so on until you progress to within 10 mm (0·4 in.) of the edge of the work. Each row of hammer blows must overlap if the work is to retain a reasonably true edge without waves or bumps. It is also important, with each new course of raising, to move the work towards you so that you always keep the point of contact near the corner of your stake, and are never hitting too far in advance of it. This will prevent the work from bouncing and jarring and hurting your hand. It should be possible to raise holding the work with only a finger and thumb, providing your technique is correct.

The stance of the craftsman, seated or standing, is important during raising. Hold the metal in one hand which will often be in contact with the side of the stake as raising proceeds, and thrust the shoulder on that side forward. The hammer, the hand that holds it, the forearm, elbow, and shoulder, should line up with the axis of the raising stake and the work for maximum accuracy. A craftsman working at a vice on a bench may sit on the bench and put his feet on a stool. During a big raising the outside of the leading knee may touch the work lightly and act as an aid to accurate positioning; it should not act as a brace against the metal bouncing or jarring. As the edge of the work is approached some craftsmen prefer to remove the remaining crinkles and pleats with a hide mallet, but careful work with the metal raising hammer is probably the best method. The dangers to be avoided at this stage include excessive thinning of the edge, a build-up of pleats that can become cracks which will need constant re-soldering, and possible damage to the surface of the raising stake as a result of wild hammering.

After each course of raising, and before annealing, the edge of the work may be caulked to build up its thickness. Hold the work, mouth uppermost, on a sandbag and hammer the edge with a raising or collet hammer. Each course of caulking will gradually thicken the metal. The technique is invaluable when a design calls for a strong, good-looking edge, unbroken by the addition of a thickening wire.

As raising proceeds check the shape of the work regularly against the design elevation, using either a purely visual judgement, or by taking measurements, or using a cardboard or aluminium template. Under no circumstances should a flare be allowed to develop on the sides of the work during raising. This happens when too much metal is taken in at the start of a raising course, and it becomes impossible to sustain the effort as far as the edge. Should a flare develop, remove it by starting the next course of raising high on the side of the body.

The inexperienced craftsman often finds difficulty in raising metal when the work has reached the stage at which its sides are angled at 45°. This problem can be solved by starting the next raising high up on the side, the following one a course lower, and so on until raising can continue normally. Check the work regularly to make sure that it is true around its vertical axis. If it leans or bulges make sure you are working from an accurate centre, and that you are using the circles as an aid to accuracy. In the case of extreme inaccuracy you may need to raise on the offending

Fig. 19 Caulking the edge of an object to strengthen it

Fig. 20 Wooden creasing block

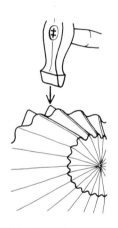

Fig. 21 Creasing

side only, but usually a careful concentration on accurate work will save you. If you are reasonably experienced you may attempt to raise asymetric forms by deliberately working from an off-centre point. This is not easy and requires great concentration and care.

A craftsman may be unlucky enough to experience cracks in the metal that he is raising, and they fall into two main categories. The first is seen as metal fatigue, which produces a myriad of interlocking cracks which develop into a jagged hole; it has its roots in incorrect annealing. Silver will break up swiftly if it is seriously over-heated, and metal which is under-heated or not annealed after each course of raising may suffer the same fate, albeit more slowly. In serious cases of over-heating, especially in the early stages of a deep raising, be ruthless and scrap your metal. The second category of cracks occurs when pleats are formed, sometimes as a result of attempting to raise too much metal at a time. The craftsman, unable to smooth them out, folds the metal onto itself. The fold eventually becomes a crack that can be soldered with a hard solder, but may prove a source of trouble for the rest of the raising.

A technique which may be used by an experienced craftsman as an aid to fast raising is creasing. Before each raising lay the work out with radial pencil lines and select a collet hammer with a well rounded face. Prepare a wood block with a groove of up to 15 mm (0·59 in.) deep and up to 12 cm (4·75 in.) long in the end grain. Place the blank over the wood block. Hammer the metal into the groove in the wood, working on a radial line. Start with light blows from the collet hammer at the point at which raising will commence, and work to the outer edge. Increase the power of your hammering so that the crease widens and deepens towards the edge of the blank. Hammer similar grooves all round the blank, using the radial lines as a guide to accuracy. Then anneal the metal, scribe circles on the outer surface, and begin a normal raising. Creasing may precede each raising as long as a creasing block can be inserted into the work. Flaring on the sides of the work is caused by hammering grooves too deeply in the centre of the metal. To rectify the fault, begin the next course of creasing high up the side of the work. Whichever technique you employ take great care over the final course, when the form is finalized and the surface smoothed as much as possible to make subsequent planishing easier.

It should be mentioned, too, that even though you have been advised to work to an accurate design elevation the final three-dimensional form may well prove to be imperfect in one respect or another. Do not hesitate to undertake improvements at this stage.

5 Seaming

Seaming may be used to produce forms of all sizes, shapes and proportions, including deep cylinders and cones, small jewelry settings for cabochon stones and the conical forms from which claw settings may be cut. Copper, gilding metal, silver and gold are all suitable materials for this technique. The gauge of metal will vary according to the design and scale of the project, but generally speaking 0·9 mm (0·036 in.) is employed in most holloware. Where more weight is required 1·092 mm (0·043 in.) might well be used. A cabochon setting might employ 0·610 mm (0·024 in.) or even thinner for very small stones. Where economy of material is necessary, thickening wires may be incorporated around the rim and base of vessels (see Chapter 10).

You must calculate the metal blank for a seamed project with reference to an accurate, full size, design drawing; often you will find you have to project a geometric development. The calculation for a straight-sided cylinder is simple. Measure the height for one dimension, and for the other multiply the diameter by 3. Subsequent forming and hammering operations will true the cylinder and expand it to the designed diameter.

Conical forms are the basis of many seamed designs. Calculate the shape of the blank with the aid of a tracing of the full-size design elevation. Fig. 22 suggests the approximate conical forms for a variety of designs – some involving a certain amount of raising after seaming and trueing, and others requiring a little stretching.

To calculate the blank for a given cone refer to fig. 23 and proceed as follows. ABCD represents the cone. Produce AB and CD to meet at E. With E as compass centre and EA as the radius describe an arc through and beyond A and C. Extend the compass radius to EB and describe an arc through and beyond BD. Set compasses to radius BD and with D and B as centres mark I and G. Join IE and GE. The figure HIGF represents the blank from which a cone with the side elevation ABDC may be made.

A design may require a combination of separate cones, or cylinders and cones, but the implications of a form which comprises several seamed components should be carefully considered. When the components are soldered together there is a danger of their seams opening, so spoiling the job, and entailing at the very least time-consuming repairs. It might be better to raise each component separately.

The shape of a blank should be scribed on the metal with the aid of trisquares, rulers, dividers, and scribers. In the case of a cone a template of the development might help. All blanks with straight edges are best cut with a treadle guillotine, but of course most people have only shears

Fig. 22 Seaming blanks. Dotted lines represent the profile of the form. When seamed, the blank will have to be raised to the designed shape

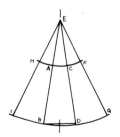

Fig. 23 Calculating a blank for seaming

available, in which case the work is made easier if one handle of the shears is held in a vice, and the other is operated by hand with the weight of the body applying further pressure. You should cut concave curves with a piercing saw or a band saw. Trim the blank with a file after shearing, to remove sharp and dangerous edges, and, of course, smooth away any imperfections of form.

Mallets with wood, horn or nylon heads may be used. It is vital to keep the hammering faces in perfect condition. Constant use breaks the surface of any mallet, and unless it is occasionally smoothed with a file or abrasive paper, it will damage the surface of soft metal, involving you in hours of tedious repair work during the finishing stages.

The metal blank may be worked into a cylinder over an iron or steel bar of appropriate diameter – about 13 mm (0·5 in.) less than that of the proposed cylinder. A conical body must be malleted over an appropriate tapered mandrel. A good workshop should possess a range of bars 8–10 cm (3–4 in.) in diameter, a large bench mandrel, one or two smaller mandrels, and a ring triblet for holding in a vice.

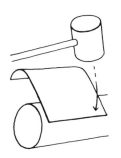

Fig. 24   Malleting a blank to form a cylinder

In forming any seamed body, conical or cylindrical, first mallet the opposite edges of the blank, which will become the joint, to approximately the correct curve (fig. 24). Should the blank be shaped into a cylindrical form by working from one edge towards the other, you will find it hard to curve the last inch or two because of lack of leverage and difficulty in gripping the blank.

Having curved the joint edges of the blank, continue the process with the centre section to bring the edges together, trying if possible to bend the metal over the mandrel with hand pressure, and using the mallet as sparingly as possible. The seam ends may not easily close up, and it may be necessary to mallet the metal from some way back from the seam, working towards the joint edge.

It is impossible to make a seamed blank truly circular or even oval, as required by a design, until the joint is soldered. As long as the plane of the metal across the joint flows smoothly (fig. 25) it does not matter if the rest of the body is comparatively misshapen.

Fig. 25   The correct and the incorrect joint for a seam

The joint edges will almost certainly not form a perfect joint, and they should be sprung apart sufficiently to insert a flat file, with which all ill-fitting areas may be removed. The work is now ready to be soldered, but should first be annealed to remove all the tensions that the previous operation will have set up in the metal. Such tensions, if not removed, may cause a joint to open during the early stages of soldering. After annealing, clean the joint edges with a file or abrasive cloth. The edges may be nicked with the edge of a square or triangular file. The solder tends to 'key' into the nicks, strengthening the joint. Press the joint edges together and then spring them past each other so that they remain overlapped. Carefully pull them slightly apart and allow them to spring together, face to face, to make a tight joint.

For seamed holloware, use binding wire to hold the joint together during heating. There should be at least one twisted loop in each piece of binding wire, in addition to the twisted ends which fasten the wire around the body. The loops and the twisted ends may be twisted even more to tighten the wire, in addition to the twisted ends which fasten the wire around the body. The loops and the twisted ends may be twisted even more to tighten the wire around the body so that the seam does not open under heat. Either the twisted ends or the loop should be located over the joint (fig. 26), because they form a small 'bridge' which may prevent the solder running away from the joint and along the wire, fastening it to the surface of the work. Should the wire become soldered to the body, remove it by rolling it off with a pair of round-nosed pliers (fig. 27). Do not wrench or file it except as a last resort. Space the binding wire along the length of the body at approximately 4 cm (1·5 in.) intervals. When binding cones (fig. 28), attach at least three vertical wires, each with evenly spaced loops along their length, to the body, one on either side of, and one opposite, the seam. Bend the ends of the wires over the top and bottom edges of the blank to hold them in place. The wires which will hold the seam tightly together must pass through the loops in the vertical wires or be caught under them, so that when tension is applied by twisting the ends together, the wire will not slide up the cone and off at the narrow end. In the case of small holloware or jewelry seams binding wire is often not used, the joint being merely sprung together. In general, the thinner the gauge of metal in relation to the diameter of the body, the more likely the seam is to open under heat, and the more necessary it is to use wire.

Fig. 26 Twist binding wire over a seam

Before heating, apply borax to the joint, which you should have already cleaned scrupulously. When soldering seams in holloware, place the work upright in the centre of the hearth; the seam will be vertical. Heat the work at first with a large, all-enveloping, soft flame while slowly revolving the hearth. As soon as the work is basically warmed, reduce the flame a little, stop revolving the hearth and apply the heat to the back of the work, opposite the seam. This seems to remove stresses and ensures that the joint does not open when heat is applied directly to it. When the metal has begun to redden, revolve the hearth and apply heat directly to the joint. Quite a bright red must be reached before enamelling (800°C) or hard (775°C) stick solder, held in tongs, can be applied to the joint. The flame may be reduced as the solder is applied, so that it does not melt too soon. Should the heat of the work drop below the melting point of the solder, as often happens, build it up again with a large flame. It is a mistake during any soldering operation to use a flame into which too much air is blown. Such a flame makes a very impressive noise, but tends to oxidize the borax and the surface of the metal, and although the correct heat appears to have been reached, the solder does not run freely. Apply the solder to the top and bottom of the joint. Then apply it downwards from the top. When you have soldered the joint, lay the work on the hearth on its back with the joint uppermost, and make good any solder deficiencies. Only a small part of the joint should be molten at any one time so that there is no danger of the seam moving.

Fig. 27 Remove binding wire from a soldered seam with round-nosed pliers

Now cool the work in cold water, and, after removing all binding wire, place it in hot pickle to remove oxides and borax. When the work is clean it should be washed in water. Remove any lumps of solder carefully with a file, but before the whole joint is cleaned you should mallet it along its length on a suitable bar or mandrel. This action will eliminate any un-

Fig. 28 Wiring a seamed cone for soldering

evenness in the lining up of the joint edges.

After malleting, the joint should be finally cleaned with a file, using great care not to thin the metal too much or to spread the file marks too far around the body. When filing is completed stone the work in preparation for planishing (see Chapter 9).

You can also solder a seam joint with the solder cut into small pieces, called paillons or panels, which are placed on the joint prior to heating. This method may appeal to beginners or to those who dislike soldering with a stick. The work should be boraxed, wired if appropriate, and laid on its side, joint downwards. Enamelling or hard solder should be cut into squares of 1·5–2 mm (0·059–0·079 in.) according to the size of the work to be soldered. The solder should then be placed along the joint inside the body, spaced at 5–10 mm (0·197–0·393 in.) intervals. Place the work on the hearth and build the heat up slowly with a large, soft flame. Work the flame under the metal as much as possible as well as over the top until you have a good red heat and the solder starts to melt. At this stage you will have to direct the flame into first one end of the work, and then the other, because direct heat helps the solder to run more freely. When the solder has run, turn the work over, seam uppermost, and apply more solder on the outside if it is needed.

The techniques are similar for making seams in jewelry, but everything is done on a much smaller scale, and the pieces of solder may be applied with tweezers when the preliminary heating has taken place. Cut solder into extremely small pieces, always bearing in mind that a small component is difficult to clean up, and is much more easily spoiled, both from a practical and an aesthetic point of view, than a large piece of holloware. Such a seam is usually cleaned up with a needle file followed by water of Ayr stone or emery polishing paper.

6   Bending and Folding Sheet Metal

This chapter is concerned with techniques used in the production of boxes and many other items or components of holloware and jewelry where design work demands folded or bent metal.

The metals which may be used include copper, gilding metal, nickel, stainless steel, silver, and gold. The gauge of metal may be determined by the use to which the end product is to be put, by the cost of the chosen metal, or by its strength. In the case of holloware the range of gauges can vary from 0·71 mm (0·028 in.) to 1·63 mm (0·064 in.) while for jewelry the metal may be as thin as 0·41 mm (0·016 in.).

The tools used for folding and bending include folding bars, round steel bars of various diameters, the inevitable collection of wood blocks, a box-wood mallet, scrapers made from old files, two or three G-cramps, and, in a luxury workshop, a pantagraph engraving machine, a milling machine, or a bending press.

To bend a piece of metal in the simplest effective way, scribe a line where the bend is to take place, clamp the metal between wood blocks with the scribed line showing a little above the wood, but exactly parallel to it, and push the projecting area of metal over to the required angle with the aid of a third wood block (fig. 29). This piece of wood ensures that you apply an even pressure over the surface of the metal and do not distort or twist the flat surface. On no account should a mallet be used directly on the metal surface because dents from each blow will spoil the flat plane. Instead, place the wood block over the metal and work the mallet carefully backwards and forwards along its surface. This type of bending gives a rounded corner with a light-catching radius, rather than a razor-sharp edge. Variations of the corner radius may be achieved by rounding the edge of the wood block over which the metal is to be bent.

Different metals and different thicknesses of metal will bend with different curves. Thin gilding metal will bend with a very tight and precise radius, the same gauge in stainless steel not quite so tight. A heavy gauge in gilding metal will bend to a softer radius, whilst stainless steel of a similar gauge may be almost impossible to bend at all. A wide piece of metal is also difficult to bend and will bend to a bigger radius than a narrow piece of the same gauge. You will therefore realize that there are practical design considerations to be taken into account when exploiting bent metal.

It is also possible to bend metal by hand with folding bars. These are especially useful if you want to bend long lengths of metal or to combine several consecutive bends to make, for instance, a triangular or square vase, a condiment set, a coffee pot or jug body. The metal should be slotted

Fig. 29   Bending sheet metal held in a vice between wood pads, and applying pressure with another piece of wood

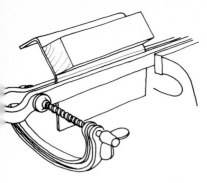

Fig. 30 Bending sheet metal
in folding bars with the aid
of a G-cramp and a vice

into the folding bars with the scribed bending line positioned slightly higher than, but in line with, the top surface of the bar. The blank must be shorter in width than the folding bars so that the open end of the bars can be placed in a vice and clamped tight, while the other end of the bar is clamped tight with a G-cramp (fig. 30). The metal blank is now held firmly and may be bent using hand pressure with the aid of a block of wood laid over it. The main problem in bending metal with the aid of folding bars is that you really need more than two hands to hold the metal in place, support the bars, and tighten the vice. I always position the blank between the bars, after first opening the vice slightly more than is necessary, and, holding the bars and blank tightly together with both hands, slide the open end of the bars into the vice. One knee should be lifted and used to swing the vice handle to tighten the jaws just a little, which leaves one hand free to adjust the blank if necessary and the other to support the projecting end of the bar and to stop the blank from slipping down. The vice can finally be tightened with one hand while you support the projecting parts of the bars and the blank with the other.

The methods described so far have one disadvantage in that metal that is clamped bends with a slightly uneven curve; however, if after each bending action the metal is turned round and clamped on the other side of the bend, an equal curve is produced.

The folding techniques discussed so far allow the production of a wide variety of designs in which the rounded corners contribute much to the look of the finished objects. A variety of configurations illustrated in fig. 31 include square boxes with two pointed and two rounded corners; boxes with three sides linked by two rounded corners with the fourth side soldered in place to give two sharp corners; and triangular boxes with two sides linked with a curved corner, and with one flat side soldered on to give sharp corners. Variations of plan forms can ring interesting changes, squares changing to diamond forms, equilateral triangles to isosceles triangles. All that the designer needs is a sketch book, a lively mind, and some paper or card to make models.

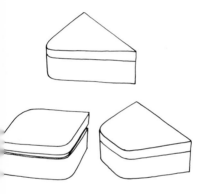

Fig. 31 Three basic ideas
to show how bent metal can
be used to produce boxes

Another simple method of bending involves the use of a metal bar of an appropriate size. The bar should be held in the vice with a good, clean length projecting at one side and the metal blank should be scribed to indicate the point at which the bend is to take place. Place a wood block on either side of the scribed line, leaving a little space between them (fig. 32). Grip the metal and wood blocks, a hand on either side, palms on the wood, fingers wrapped around the edges and under the metal, place the metal on the bar, lining up the scribed line over the centre of the bar, press downwards with the palms of the hands and bend the metal to the appropriate angle. You will get a nice natural bend and can produce other curves with the aid of different bars. This is the ideal method for producing a softer curve; the wood block or folding bars tend to produce sharper angles, although if one corner of a wood block is rounded the metal may be bent around it to produce a softer curve. Throughout this chapter I have advocated hand pressure as a forming power, and would like to emphasize that silversmithing is not all hammering. The hammer or mallet can prove a damaging weapon, distorting crisp, flat, forms with bruises

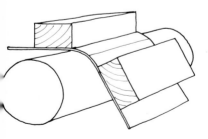

Fig. 32 Bending sheet metal
over a metal bar using wood
pressure pads

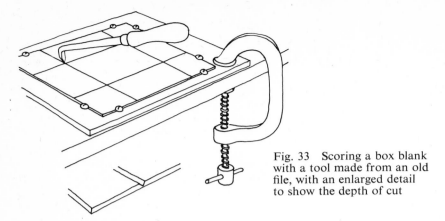

Fig. 33 Scoring a box blank with a tool made from an old file, with an enlarged detail to show the depth of cut

and hollows, and ruining a fine design.

The other major method of producing a bent or folded form is by scoring or scraping away a V section of metal, nearly cutting through the sheet, bending the metal until the angle is closed up, and then soldering the joint. The result is a sharp corner, the angle of which is controlled by the angle and width of the V that is scored or scraped away. The equipment required for this technique is very simple: a few flat pieces of hard and soft wood, a G-cramp or two, some wood screws, square and triangular needle files, and a scraper.

All metals, except steel, and nickel because it tends to warp badly under heat, may be used with this technique. Financial, practical, and aesthetic requirements will dictate the thickness of metal that should be used, but don't attempt large boxes using thin metal because the surfaces may warp during heating and will be quite impossible to correct.

The scraper (fig. 34) is made by heating the handle tang of an old file to a red heat, bending it to a right angle 13 mm (0·5 in.) from the point and then grinding the point. Harden the cutting point by heating it to a red heat and immediately quenching it in cold water or in oil. Now brighten the cutting end with emery cloth and then using a small flame, heat the tool at a point 13 mm (0·5 in.) away from the cutting edge. The tool will change colour as it is heated, and bands of colour will creep along the surface from the heating point. The cutting point will become pale yellow, then straw colour, and when it becomes brown-yellow it will be tempered to the correct degree of hardness for a scraper, and should immediately be quenched in water.

The blank of metal should now be cut. Scribe a deep line at the point where it will be bent. Fasten the metal in the centre of a flat piece of wood using screws placed on either side of each corner. The screws should be round-headed, and the heads should overlap the metal to hold it down on to the wood. Do not tighten the screws too much or the edges and the surface of the metal blank will be distorted and damaged. Fasten the wood block, with the metal blank attached, to the work bench with a G-cramp, ensuring that the scribed line lies at right angles to the edge of the bench. If you are right-handed, grip the scraper at the opposite end to the cutting point with the right hand, thumb uppermost, and place the palm of the left hand over the scraper and near to the cutting end. Put the

Fig. 34 Side and front elevation of scoring tool

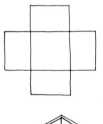

Fig. 35 Plan of blank and perspective of finished box with a solid bottom. Bottom to be fitted later

28

cutting point on to the scribed line near the far edge of the blank, apply downward pressure with the left hand and carefully draw the scraper towards yourself with the right hand. If the scraper deviates from the scribed line, turn the wood block around and proceed to scrape from the other side. Deviations are unsightly and undesirable and do not occur with experience. It may be possible to erase them with a stone if they are not too deep; as a last resort, fill them with solder. If the mistake is inside a box which is to be lined, it can be concealed by the lining and you have only to live with your conscience!

Scraping should continue until the metal is nearly cut through. You will know when to stop cutting if you take the metal off the wood block and inspect the underside. If a ridge is showing under the scraped groove, it is time to bend the metal. Place the metal on the work bench with the scraped groove lined up with the edge of the bench. Grip the metal with one hand on either side; with the fingers on the top surface press upwards with the thumbs on the underside of the metal. If you have scraped deeply enough the metal will bend very easily, but if you sense resistance to pressure, return immediately to more scraping. If you persist in bending an insufficiently scored piece of metal the corner will be neither sharp nor rounded, and furthermore the scored line will not close up, leaving an unsightly and weak inner corner. Sharp corners on a narrow strip of metal or in flat wire may be achieved by filing away the appropriate V section, instead of using a scraper. This is when a square or a triangular file is used. The files may also be used near the end of a scraped line because you may prefer to scrape more lightly towards the edge of the metal so as not to damage it when the scraper drops over the edge and digs into the wood.

The marking out of a box is critical if you are to achieve absolute accuracy, and especially if you do not intend to use a hinge. The lid will have to fit four different ways if it is square, three if it is triangular, and two if it is rectangular – a great test of accuracy. The flattened development of a box should be marked out on the metal. Work from one established straight edge, using a trisquare to mark all lines that need to be at right angles to the edge, and a metal ruler to mark and measure all lines that are parallel to the prepared edge. When you have finished scribing, check the opposite corners of the rectangle with dividers. If the measurements are equal, all angles are square and scraping may proceed. Each line should be scraped only a little at a time, because where scraped lines cross each other a hole may be made when the point of the scraper drops into, and catches in, a deep groove.

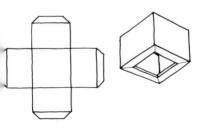

Fig. 36 Plan of blank and under-view of box with lid and sides plus a bottom flange

There are two basic box configurations; the lids of both are made as an integral part and cut off later. One configuration involves the marking and scoring of a lid and sides on one piece of metal, cutting out the corner pieces, folding up the sides after chamfering the edges to 45°, soldering all joints, and then cutting out and letting in a separate bottom sheet of metal with chamfered edges. The second method involves marking out and scoring on one piece of metal the box top and sides, with the addition of a flange on each side (fig. 36). The corner squares are cut out, and each end of the sides chamfered, while the corners of each bottom flange are cut to an angle of 45°. The whole blank is then bent up and soldered, resulting in a box with a lid, sides, a flange all around the bottom and a large hole in the centre bottom. The bottom of the box may be completed with a loose metal sheet, held in place by a wood liner, or simply with a wood liner.

In soldering the scored and bent angles of a box, observe a strict routine. Difficulties in soldering usually result in panic and overheating, which in turn result in the warped surfaces which are fatal to a box. The box must first be wired with an annular wire around the sides to pull all the corner joints tight. Loop the wire at three of the four corners and join the ends at the fourth. This allows the wire to be tensioned from each corner, and prevents the wire cutting into and damaging the sharp corners. All the joints should be well boraxed, and you must cut a large number of small squares or paillons of hard solder. Using a pair of tweezers, place the paillons of solder at intervals of 6 mm (0·25 in.) all around the inner bottom corner of the box. Now place a steel mesh or ribbed hearth brick on to the hearth turntable and heat it well with the soldering torch. The mesh or the ribs on the brick will allow the flame to heat the bottom of the box when you start soldering and the pre-heated hearth aids this process. When the hearth is hot place the box in the centre and heat it with a large, soft flame, watching the borax and the solder paillons all the time. When the borax shows signs of boiling and displacing the solder, remove the flame for a second or so. Constantly pass the flame back and forth across the box, revolving the hearth all the time. As the borax settles down you may inject more air into the flame and bring the box to a dull red heat. Each corner may be soldered using a stick of very hard solder held in tongs; with luck the hard solder inside the box will run at the same time. It may be necessary to cut the flame size a little and direct it into the box and directly on to the solder paillons, but take care because an intense heat may cause the lid to expand and warp. If you have to direct the flame into the box, point it along a side rather than at right angles. This spreads the heat more evenly and helps the solder to run.

When a complete bottom plate is to be soldered into a box it is first fitted by chamfering the edges and those of the box sides. This is an exacting job and you must take your time, making sure that all the angles are filed most accurately. Before you start soldering, the line where the lid will be cut off must be marked on the box sides with the aid of a scribing block or a metal ruler and scriber. Now, using a back saw or a piercing saw, cut a slit along the lid parting line at one corner of the box so that when the bottom is being soldered in place hot, expanding air can escape from the enclosed box, and when the soldering is finished and the air cools and contracts, more air can enter, thus preventing any bulging or collapsing. When you are satisfied that the job is ready for soldering, borax all jointing surfaces, fit the bottom and wire it into place with wires running across the box, and along its length, making sure that there is a twisted loop at each corner (fig. 37). Pre-heat the hearth and then solder the joint using hard or medium solder. After soldering take the box from the hearth, using tongs, and place it somewhere safe to cool. Do not put it into acid before cutting the lid off. When it is cool renew the scribed line marking

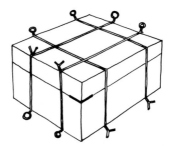

Fig. 37 Box with top wired into place prior to soldering. Note saw cut at front corner to allow air to escape during heating, and to enter on cooling

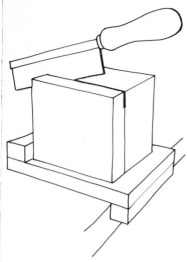

Fig. 38 Lid being sawn off on a bench sawing block

the joint between lid and box, and with a back saw or piercing saw, starting from the corner that is already pierced, start to saw the lid off (fig. 38). Do not put the box in a vice, but hold it with hand pressure, perhaps using a jig like a woodworker's bench sawing block. Take your time; if you try to force the pace the saw will jump out of the slit and gash the sides of the box.

When you have finished sawing inspect the edges of the box and the lid and test them for crooked and wavy edges by placing them open end downwards on a flat surface. Mark any bumps with a pencil and file them off, constantly re-testing on the flat surface. Do not use a mechanical emery band or linisher. At best it will take off too much metal or buckle the sides, and at worst the box may be torn from your hands and smashed against a wall.

Boxes with bent sides, discussed above, may well have cut-off lids, and will also have both tops and bottoms chamfered and soldered into the bodies. Fig. 39 illustrates possible constructional details.

It is possible to solder bottoms and tops of boxes using a simple butt joint and no chamfering. This faster method may appeal but remember that surplus metal will have to be filed off, that the sides of the box will inevitably become scratched, and that when the box is finished and polished a faint joint line may show where the softer solder has worn away.

Important design variations can be introduced into boxes by using wires to give different lid fittings; these are described in Chapter 10.

Fig. 39 Box with chamfered bottom ready for soldering

Fig. 40 Box with projecting bottom wired and ready for soldering

7 Forming: sheet metal

This chapter aims to offer guidance on the production of a variety of sheet metal forms in which the technique and the estimation of the blanks is not quite so straightforward as in raising, seaming, or sinking, though the basic principles may well be the same.

The tools include collet hammers and doming hammers of various sizes. Recourse may also be made to raising hammers and wood or horn mallets. Metal is often formed into and over wood blocks which are cut, carved and rasped to shape. The tree trunk with a variety of hollows in the upper surface and a variety of concave grooves cut around the edge is an incredibly versatile tool. Lead blocks may be used for stamping where the limited repetition of a form is required, such as in a spoon bowl or a short run of jewelry. In these cases the male dies may be made from large bolt heads.

Saddle stakes, or old round files, softened, bent to shape and polished, or saddle shapes cut and filed from thick sheet or slab steel can all prove extremely useful.

Gilding metal, copper, silver, and gold may be employed in gauge thicknesses ranging from 0·61–1·30 mm (0·024–0·051 in.). Sheet stainless steel may be beaten into versions of the forms discussed below but its hardness may cause damage to stakes and hammers alike.

Estimating blanks for complex, duo-curve forms such as spouts, is not as straightforward as estimating blanks for raised beakers or sunken dishes. In most cases it is best to make a very accurate model of the component from which the blank, or blanks, of metal may be calculated. A sheet metal profile should be cut and an exact model (fig. 45) be constructed around it, using modelling clay or Plasticine. It is best to build up the form as a sculptor would, rolling small pellets between thumb and forefinger and applying them gradually to build the exact contours. Squeezing, squashing, and scraping an oversize lump of modelling medium is an unsatisfactory and inaccurate method and should not be practised. In the case of a handle or spout it is a good idea to place the model on the main body at some time during the final stages of modelling, because the form, size, and all proportions of the two must be satisfactorily related. It will also be possible to confirm if practical requirements, such as comfortable lifting for a handle, are going to be met. Remember that the pouring lip of a spout should be at least 1 mm (0·0394 in.) higher than the highest proposed level of liquid in the pot.

It is now necessary to describe in detail the development of a blank. Let us assume we are producing a D-section tea or coffee pot spout.

Fig. 41   Collet hammer

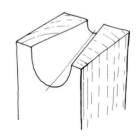

Fig. 42   Wood block into which spout blank is hammered

Fig. 43   Old file bent and polished for use as a stake

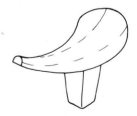

Fig. 44   Saddle stake

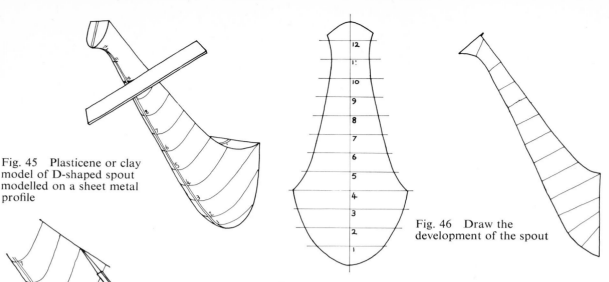

Fig. 45   Plasticene or clay model of D-shaped spout modelled on a sheet metal profile

Fig. 46   Draw the development of the spout

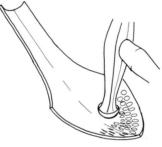

Fig. 47   Measure spout dimensions

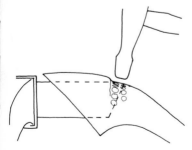

Fig. 48   The lower end of the spout being hollowed to shape

Fig. 49   The lower end of the spout being raised to shape

The metal profile upon which the model has been built forms a useful central datum line. On the underbelly of the model, and along this datum line, use dividers to mark off consecutive numbered points, each 1 cm (0·394 in.) apart. The edge of a straight metal strip or a ruler should be pressed into the model at each point in turn. With a rocking motion mark a line around the curve and at a tangent to the profile of the spout.

On a piece of paper draw a vertical line divided by 12 horizontal numbered lines spaced at 1 cm (0·394 in.) intervals. Use this drawing to mark out the development of the lower curved surface of the spout. At point 1 on the model measure the diagonal distance between where the impressed line intersects with the central datum line and where it terminates at the edge of the top surface (fig. 47). This distance should be marked off at point 1 on the drawing, first on one side of the datum line, and then on the other. Now measure at point 2 and so on down the spout. Join all consecutive points on each side of the vertical centre to obtain the development of the spout.

Take a tracing and use it to mark out the metal by sticking it to the surface, tracing through carbon paper, or pricking around the outline with a scriber. Cut around the outline with shears or a piercing saw (I prefer the latter). After trimming the edge with a file, anneal the blank and scribe a centre line on each side so that as forming proceeds, you can check the accuracy of the form at regular intervals. At this stage you will need a collet hammer and doming hammer together with scrap wood, in whose end-grain grooves and hollows may be cut using a woodworker's rasp and a gouge. The tree trunk mentioned earlier in the chapter might fulfill most of these requirements. The lower end of the spout may be formed by hammering the blank over a hollow in wood using a regular and symmetrical hammer pattern around the centre line (fig. 48). Alternatively, it may be raised on a suitable stake (fig. 49), or more usually, a combination of the two techniques may be employed. The lower end will not be fully shaped after one course of hammering, but rather than anneal the blank and work the same area again, proceed to work the upper part of the spout, hammering the metal into a shallow groove in wood

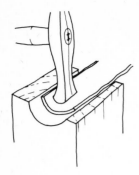

Fig. 50   Hammer the spout
blank into a wood block

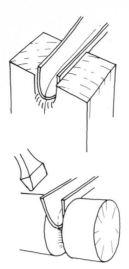

Fig. 51   Flare the spout end
in a wood block (above) or
into a grooved wooden dowel
(below)

Fig. 52   Handle blank with
wire soldered strap to
prevent the form opening out
during hammering

with a suitable collet hammer. The whole spout, now partially shaped, will be work-hardened at this stage and should be annealed. Check the blank for twists and inaccuracies, which should be removed by twisting the metal by hand, or manipulating it by pressing it against the bench or the tree trunk. Renew the centre lines on the blank and repeat the hammering processes, deepening the hollows and grooves in the wood as work proceeds, selecting narrower hammers where needed, and checking and correcting inaccuracies as they occur. Look along the length of the spout to check for twists, and check regularly with your drawing. Should a spout need narrowing, lie it first on one side, and then the other, tapping along the length with a horn mallet.

During the production of spouts, hollow bracelets, or handles the metal will resist being formed. When you are shaping the profile, the section will open out, but when you are deepening the section, the profile will tend to straighten out. Especially difficult is the inside section of a handle, because the metal is being forced in opposite directions. The sheet should be bent to the profile form first, and should be hollowed a little at a time. Restore the profile shape before each course of hollowing and deepen the wooden former as you go. It is possible to prevent a handle profile from straightening by temporarily soldering a metal strap between the ends (fig. 52). Remove it when planishing is completed. It sometimes helps to use a saddle stake, a bent bar, or an old, round file, working the metal into the curve with a collet hammer.

In general, proceed cautiously, do not try to do too much too quickly, anneal the metal often and check constantly against distortion and twisting.

34

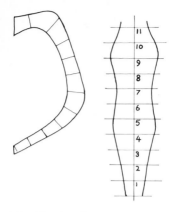

Fig. 53   Profile of handle together with its development

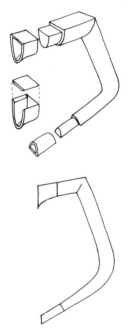

Fig. 54   Solid handle and exploded diagram of metal sockets

Planishing is described in Chapter 9, but it is worth emphasizing that regular checks should be made to ensure that the form does not open in all directions as planishing proceeds, and worth warning also that it is often necessary to return to some careful forming operations to correct distortions. The principles of these processes can be applied to a wide variety of forms, including hollow handles. Simple, logical modifications to the drafting process will allow the designer to arrive at the development of almost any form.

A solid wood, ivory, fibre or plastic handle will often fit into metal sockets, which are in turn soldered to the main body. In such a case it is a good idea to make the handle first, and then if necessary to file away a rebate at each end of the handle to allow the sockets to fit flush with the handle profile. Model the sockets on the handle, fit to the main body, and then calculate the socket developments. When the sockets have been made they should be placed on the handle and fitted to the main body. When you have achieved a good fit, hold the handle and sockets in place on the body and use a scriber to mark their positions accurately. Cut stitches to the scribed lines, lay the body on its side on the hearth, place the sockets in position within the stitches, and complete the soldering. The handle should then fit perfectly.

A spout or hollow handle may have a circular, oval, or egg-shaped section; I prefer to make such a form in two parts. A spout might be said to have two main surfaces – a top and a bottom – while a hollow handle has an inside and an outside surface. Each curved surface must have a development plotted with the aid of a model and by the methods described above. For the spout the lower part must be made first, and for the handle the inside form. After planishing the form trim the edges and file them to size; then make the upper part to fit.

When soldering spout sections together adapt the wiring technique used for a seamed cone (see Chapter 5) to prevent the wiring slipping down the taper. This technique is exacting but because two halves are involved it is possible to achieve a perfect form. This is not so easy when a spout is made in one piece because it is almost impossible to work the whole form on metal stakes, which play a large part in forming an exact shape.

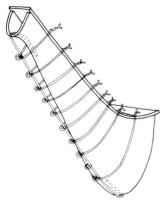

Fig. 55   Spout wired for soldering

35

Fig. 56   Block in which
lead-filled spout is being bent

Fig. 57   Lead-filled spout
being planished on a sandbag

A one-piece spout should also be planned as a seamed cone, using a model to determine the dimensions of the blank. Having constructed the cone, mix a thick rouge or whitening solution, coat the cone inside and leave it to dry. Embed one end in dry sand or plug it with a hard wood bung and pour in molten lead. The blank may now be slowly shaped into grooves in wood, or by inserting it into a shaped slot in hard wood and easing it round (fig. 56). It may be necessary to melt the lead out of the spout at intervals and then to anneal it. Melt the lead out at the lowest possible temperature to avoid contaminating or burning the spout wall; inspect the spout closely for contamination. Scouring with a bottle brush and pumice powder is an additional precaution. Too swift a forming operation can result in difficult-to-remove creases in the metal surface. Some forming, and certainly most planishing, can be done while the lead-filled spout is rested on a sandbag with collet and planishing hammers (fig. 57). A similar technique may be used to produce a hollow handle, or the arm of a candelabra.

Spoon bowls and similar forms may be stamped into lead using a modified bolt head as a male die. First of all you must produce an accurate plan and elevation; then shape a bolt head to the identical form (fig. 58), and finish it with a high polish. Draw a line over the curved surface of the resultant form to represent the longitudinal axis. Divide the line into equal divisions and at each division draw a line at a tangent to the axis, extending on either side to the edge of the stake. As described in the development of a spout, draw a diagram with an axis and lines crossing it, identical in spacing and numbers to those on the stake. Take measurements as described for spoon making, join all points, and you will have the blank outline of the spoon bowl. Cut the blank out of the metal, with or without the handle, according to the requirements of the design. Strike the spoon stake into a lead block until a complete mould is impressed – it is easier

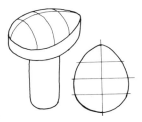

Fig. 58   Spoon stake divided
to calculate the blank
alongside

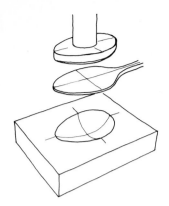

Fig. 59 Spoon stake, blank
and lead block mould
showing guide lines

to do this if the lead block is hot. Mark the longitudinal axis on the lead and on the blank; in addition mark a cross axis at the widest part of the mould and the blank. This will enable you to register the blank accurately over the mould (fig. 59). Line the mould with tissue paper, place the blank in position and strike the stake onto it with a heavy hammer. Several blows may be needed, and the blank may need annealing. If so, strike the stake into the mould before stamping the blank again. Always scrub the blank with pumice powder before annealing to remove any lead contamination. Finally true the bowl by tapping it with a horn mallet or a planishing hammer over the spoon stake which should be held in a vice.

8 Forming: forging and hammering strips and bars

The forming techniques described in this chapter relate in the main to the deformation of metal bars, round, square, and rectangular in section, to produce such items as cutlery, solid metal handles, sculptural bases, necklaces and other jewelry components. The technique gives the designer-craftsman considerable scope for achieving interesting and subtle plays of light and texture.

Collet hammers, raising hammers, and special, heavy forging hammers are used. The important characteristic of the forging hammer is that the striking face is convex on a lateral axis to the handle. When it strikes the metal it bites into the surface and has a stretching, spreading action. Each raising hammer has one such rounded face in addition to its flat raising face.

Gilding metal, copper, silver, gold, nickel silver, and steel are all suitable for forging. All metals, except steel, are worked cold, but don't forget that forging is a drastic treatment for metal, and it will need to be quickly annealed. Failure to anneal the metal often enough will result, at best, in difficulty and discomfort in moving the metal. At worst, the metal will start to disintegrate – although in certain cases this effect may be utilized, as, for instance if metal is forged until it is paper thin at the edges and allowed to develop a ragged edge. The effect is attractive and can, with careful designing, be put to decorative use.

Steel must be worked hot and, stainless steel especially, is liable to a sudden and fundamental break up if it is worked too cool. It should be reheated just as soon as the metal loses its dull red colour. Stainless steel is liable to damage in another way through incorrect heating: the stainless quality, or resistance against corrosion, can be impaired. In practice I have experienced no serious problems in a range of jewelry and cutlery applications, though no doubt the worked metal would be considered sub-standard and damaged for exacting technological purposes. From the point of view of the designer-craftsman, stainless steel has attractive qualities, the colour being not the least, but it can be hard and slow to work and finish, making it an expensive material to be involved with if sales are to be considered. In short, skilful and resourceful designing is needed.

During forging the craftsman can anneal the metal on a normal silver-smith's hearth; you need only place a few fire bricks behind the work to concentrate the heat around the metal. Non-ferrous metals should be quenched in water as in any other annealing. Steel, being worked hot, can be held in forge tongs during heating, after which a quick dash to an

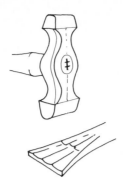

Fig. 60 Hammer used for widening metal strip

Fig. 61 Forged and tapered form

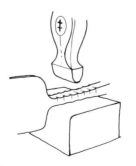

Fig. 62 Spoon handle being forged to shape

anvil will be necessary, so that the work can proceed before the metal cools too much.

The tools and stakes on which metal can be worked during forging vary depending upon the job to be done. Almost every stake in the workshop might be used, and even a hammer face can prove to be the ideal anvil. The beginner must be very careful with the forging hammer when working over well finished stakes because it is all too easy to mis-hit and damage the stake. It is often important that the stake and hammer have fine finishes, because the completed form may be most suitable for its purpose with a natural hammer finish. The stoning and polishing needed to remove surface flaws produced by damaged tools will utterly destroy the surface quality of a finished article.

At this stage it is appropriate to discuss the precise effects of the forging process. Let us consider the deformation of a round bar. To spread one end of the bar, that is to widen it, and at the same time to flatten it, it must be hammered over an anvil or flat stake with the hammer at right angles to the axis of the bar (fig. 60). Strike first of all right on top of the bar, and as it widens, hammer evenly across the surface of the metal. Watch the movement of the metal at every stage because, as the metal spreads outwards, the form will flow from the bar in a flaring shape, with tapering planes on the edges. Several satisfying, logical and well balanced forms will show themselves at various stages. As a result of such observation the designer-craftsman can amass a vocabulary of forms arising from technique, which can be made to serve other ideas.

It is a worthwhile exercise to widen each end of a bar, widening first one end, then turning the metal through a right angle, and widening the other so that the thin end of each is the edge and thickness of the other at its widest (fig. 61). Remember to work all surfaces constantly, because while one surface is being hammered, its edges may be getting ragged, and you will remain in command of the form only by switching the hammering from one surface to the other. This exercise will enable the beginner to understand just what happens when a spoon bowl runs into a handle, or perhaps a knife blade into a handle.

The secret of perfect forging is complete command of the hammer technique so that the required dimensions and surfaces are attained without recourse to time-consuming and wasteful filing and cutting. Of course the metal stretches and grows as it is hammered and there is no easy formula for estimating metal requirements as in raising or sinking. Only experience will help, though it is always safe to work from one end of a bar and measure progress constantly. Any surplus metal allows you something to hold while working, and may be cut off later.

It is often necessary to forge a narrow neck at the point where a flat plane tapers away into a handle, as in a spoon blank, and in such a case the metal may well have to be reduced in all-round bulk as well. When striking the metal, make sure the hammer handle is in line with the metal bar so that when the hammer face bites into the metal it will lengthen rather than widen it (fig. 62). The metal must be hammered systematically, and a method which involves the flattened area being held vertical for one course of hammering and held in a horizontal plane for the next is by far the best.

It is simply no good hammering here and there, turning the metal around every now and again, because a sadly misshapen form will result. The forging should take place upon a flat stake with at least one rounded edge so that when the wide flat end is held vertical it is possible to forge right up to it (see fig. 62). Remember that the metal will lengthen as it is thinned, and if it is to taper as well, it must be checked regularly against the design. Remember also to true all surfaces regularly with the hammer as you proceed. If you wish to reduce or draw down a bar to a taper, later to be made circular, forge it to a square taper, working first one face and then the other, and then knock the corners off with the hammer prior to draw filing and polishing.

Decorative bent wire work, such as may be used in jewelry, can often be 'lifted' and the curves given emphasis and rhythm by widening and flattening the wire at their apex.

Jewelry collars may also be forged and in this case the form of the collar is often required to fit the neck and shoulders, which results in an ever varying angle on the surface of the metal as it runs around the body contours. To make such a form fasten paper tightly around a dressmaker's dummy, drawing the collar accurately on paper, cut the paper where the collar opening is to be, remove the paper, and open it flat upon the bench. The result is a pattern or development of the collar. The metal should now be forged to shape; start at one end, reduce it to dimension bit by bit and produce the curves by stretching one side, or pulling it in a wood block. To convert the flat development to the three-dimensional form of the collar, bend it by hand over a tapered mandrel, or a suitable stake, malleting it only if really necessary.

Finally, because the technique of forging requires experience and time to perfect, many people will have to resort to filing and cutting to produce accurately the form and the finish that they desire – one that will stand inspection from any angle. This is a very important point: view the work constantly from *all* angles. In the case of stainless steel use various grades of 'wet and dry' sand paper after files to produce a perfect surface before you polish or put on a satin surface.

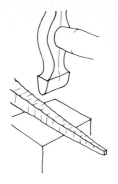

Fig. 63　Metal rod being forged to a point

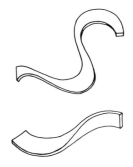

Fig. 64　Bent wires forged to different widths to emphasize curves

40

9 Planishing

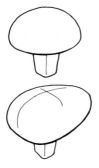

Fig. 65 Horse's head stakes

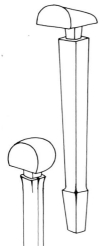

Fig. 66 Stakes held in a commercial bottom stake holder (right) and in a piece of conduit pipe (left)

Planishing, in silversmithing and jewelry, is the smoothing of metal. It is usually carried out by hammering the surface of the work on a suitably shaped and highly polished stake with a hammer whose striking face should also be highly polished. The general aim of this process is to remove all unsightly marks from the surface of the work and, by constant hammering, to develop a surface which is consistent with the qualities and requirements of the design.

Suppose we are planishing a semicircular bowl. The first and most puzzling problem is the selection of a suitable stake on which to planish the work. Remember that the form of the design should have been accurately produced during the forming process, whether it be raising, sinking, seaming, or any other method, and that therefore the shape should not be altered during the planishing process, but simply trued and refined. When planishing a semicircular bowl the stake, too, should have a semicircular form (fig. 65), though of a slightly smaller radius than that of the bowl. This will allow some movement of the bowl during the hammering process, while still ensuring that the bumps are smoothed out. A stake which is too large in radius will cause the shape of the bowl to be altered, while a stake that is too small will make it difficult to smooth the surface of the bowl. Furthermore, the inside may become deeply marked and the form may even be distorted and raised to a completely different shape.

Having selected a suitable stake fix it into a bottom stake holder (fig. 66), a horse (fig. 67), or directly into the vice, so that you can place the work over it and hammer it easily all over the surface without the edge fouling any part of the stake holder and thereby preventing a good contact between stake and bowl. Select the hammer. For the average planishing job a hammer with a 175-g (6-oz) head that has one round and one square face (fig. 68). The round face has a flat surface with a softened edge so that a mis-hit will not cut the surface of the work too badly. The square face, which is usually used to planish cylindrical and conical forms, has a convex surface whose axis runs counter to the axis of the handle. The reason why the surfaces of the hammer and stake should be highly polished is that when the work is planished the polish of the tools is reproduced on the inner and outer surfaces. Indeed, in theory it should be possible to clean the work with a cloth and metal polish when the hammering is completed and be rewarded with a fine soft finish. In practice, however, the subsequent solderings and working which are required in most designs make this an unattainable ideal.

Before you begin planishing, the work should be annealed, quenched

Fig. 67 Horse held in a vice

41

in cold water, pickled in hot acid or a proprietary pickle, washed, and then scoured with pumice powder. Then with pencil compasses scribe the outer surface of the work with concentric circles approximately 1 cm (0·5 in.) apart (fig. 69). Place the work centrally upon the stake and hold it lightly with the thumb and forefinger spread on either side of the centre point, so that a hammer blow may be placed right on the centre of the bowl. The other fingers should be splayed down the surface of the bowl to have a gentle, steadying effect, and to revolve the bowl as the hammering proceeds. The hammering should proceed rhythmically around the centre hammer blow, gradually working towards the outer edge of the bowl. Overlap each hammer blow and each row of hammer blows, using the pencilled circles as a guide. It is most important to let your hammering be guided by the circles because in this way you produce a work that is accurate and true around the vertical axis. Similarly, long dishes will be accurate in both profile and in plan form, if they are worked according to guide lines based upon the plan form.

Using these two examples as general guide, it is only a matter of common sense to work out what guide lines to use on other designs. Correct hammering produces a ringing sound, with the work trapped perfectly between hammer and stake, while incorrect hammering produces a hollow sound and distortion and denting in the surface of the metal. The beginner will often experience difficulty in obtaining perfect contact between the hammer, the work, and the stake, and only practice and concentration will bring perfection. It sometimes helps to place the hammer firmly onto the work at the point where difficulty is being experienced, thereby establishing contact with the stake, and then to hold the work lightly as you start to planish again. Repeat the procedure if necessary. Planishing is often difficult because the craftsman is physically uncomfortable, standing or sitting in a cramped or tense position. Otherwise the stake may be at the wrong angle or too high or low in the vice; check these details if you are sure you have the right stake but are still not getting a good result.

To ensure that planishing takes no longer than is necessary you must gauge the strength of your hammer blows. Should the metal surface be fairly smooth, having been malleted prior to planishing, with no cuts on either surface, the gentlest hammering that will produce a polished, faceted surface, inside and out, will be sufficient. Heavy planishing on this type of surface will only mean that further planishing will be necessary to refine the surface. Should either the inner or outer surface be deeply cut and pitted by raising or sinking hammers or the stakes, the first priority is to planish hard enough to remove these marks. It might even be necessary to anneal the metal after the first planishing, and then to hammer heavily for a second course. Once all deep marks are removed stop annealing between planishing courses, and undertake at least one extra course of planishing in circles.

Inspect the inner and outer surfaces of the work. Traces of concentric ridges will almost certainly be seen to spoil the perfection of the form. At this stage the ideal planished surface will reveal an overall, even hammer texture with no perceptible ridges running in one direction or another.

Fig. 68   Planishing hammer

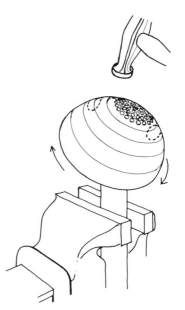

Fig. 69   Planishing a bowl. Dotted lines show position of forefinger and thumb

42

To remove concentric rings of planishing ridges, hammer the work in a radial pattern, working from the centre of the bowl to the outer edge. You may find that it helps to divide the bowl with pencil lines and shade each area as it is planished. Should it prove difficult to see where the hammer is striking on the polished surface scour the bowl with pumice powder to dull the surface. The subsequent hammering will re-polish the surface, and it will be easy to gauge progress.

After the radial planishing inspect all surfaces again. Do not anneal the metal. It may be necessary to embark upon another radial or another concentric planishing if the surface is not yet perfect. Three courses of planishing are a fortunate minimum for the average person. You may decide to polish the surface of the bowl at intervals during a planishing, and for the beginner this helps in assessing the quality of the planishing, and pinpoints where more work is necessary.

A semicircular bowl or a small shallow dish are the simplest shapes to planish because only one stake is required throughout the process. Bowls or dishes whose profiles have varying curves or whose plan forms are other than circular, and may be narrow and deep, are much more difficult. The choice of stake is once again vital to success and the beginner should consider not only matching the profile of the stake to the side elevation of the bowl, but should make sure that the curve of the cross section of the stake also fits the work form. This is essential in planishing a long, narrow dish when a long stake may be used. One that is too narrow and ridged will make a mess on the inside of the work.

The technique for planishing a long dish is different because a steady, concentric planishing in one direction only will twist and distort the form. One course in a clockwise direction, followed by one in an anti-clockwise should eliminate this problem. It may also be possible to work backwards and forwards on either side of the long axis, though each side must be worked equally or unequal tension and metal expansion will distort the form. A similar technique is employed in planishing the back and front of a two-piece spout or a hollow handle.

One of the problems that arises in planishing a long dish, or any large bowl form, is that of holding the work accurately on the stake. A small variation in the angle at which the work is held results in an alteration of the form. Don't attempt to planish a large piece of work until you have practised on several smaller pieces.

A form which has a profile of varying curves may be planished completely on one stake providing that the stake possesses a similar profile, and that you alter its angle in the vice as the planishing proceeds so that the area on which hammering is to take place is always in an accessible and comfortable position. In many cases you will need several stakes, each one fitting a particular point of the profile. It helps considerably, however, if each stake has a shape that will allow you to overlap the area of planishing produced on the preceding stake because there is always a tendency for a ridge to form at the point where one stake takes over from another. Overlapping a planishing area helps considerably, but if a ridge does develop, radial or vertical planishing, as opposed to the initial circular planishing, should eliminate it.

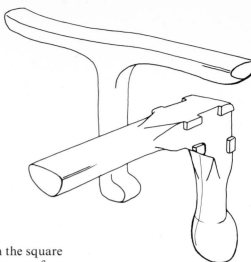

Fig. 70   Three-armed stake (above) and a jug stake

As stated earlier you should planish straight-sided pieces with the square face of the planishing hammer. The convex surface of the square face makes a circular hammer mark on a straight side. This feature is specially important when a piece of work combining globular form and straight sides is being planished, because by changing hammer faces as the form changes, a planishing mark of similar shape can be established over the whole form, thus unifying it. Furthermore, to planish a straight side with the flat-surfaced, circular hammer face requires skill and accuracy because it is easy to dig the edge of the hammer into the work. However, some people prefer the appearance of the elongated hammer mark and it may be argued that it enhances a cylindrical or conical form. In planishing a straight-sided piece of work the choice of stake is, as always, important. A polished steel bar of a diameter close to that of the work will be perfectly satisfactory, as may the straight arm of a jug stake, or of a three armed stake.

Similar stakes may be used in the planishing of trumpet forms such as beakers, though if the side of the work is very curved a stake with a concave form may be preferred, and it will be necessary to use a collet hammer (fig. 71). The head of a collet hammer has a deeper reach than that of a planishing hammer and it may also have striking faces that are more curved. It is also possible to planish a cylindrical, conical or trumpet form on a suitable stake held in a horse, though some care must be taken to see that the lower corners of the horse do not mark the inside of the work.

Fig. 71   Collet hammer

Very deep, curvilinear forms, possibly combined with straight sides, and often with narrow necks and wide lower bodies, can present the craftsman with problems. The choice of stake, and how to get it inside the work so that a good planishing contact can be made are the main considerations. Often more than one stake may be needed, and more often still it may be necessary to make a special stake. The beginner often baulks at the thought of the work involved in making and polishing a special stake, but it is often quicker, and certainly more satisfactory, than struggling with unsuitable stakes and probably finishing up with a poorly finished travesty of the required form.

Though it may seem like heresy to the master craftsman, it is sometimes worth cutting the bottom out of a very deep form that is difficult to planish, so as to gain access from either end. The justification for this is that the designed shape is all-important, and within reason any method of producing the shape is legitimate providing no structural weaknesses are introduced.

The flat bottoms of some designs can present nasty problems to the beginner, because close, concentric circle planishing from the centre outwards can cause the metal to stretch and form a 'pimple' as the planishing progresses. One way to avoid this is to planish a flat bottom using an open pattern of hammer blows; that is concentric hammering with a gap between each hammer blow and each row of hammer blows, followed by two or three similar operations which will complete the covering of the surface.

Sharp corners in a design should not be sharpened too much in the early stages of a planishing, but should be left rounded, so that if necessary slight alterations may be made. Several planishings on a very sharp corner may thin the metal and cut through it.

Hammer textures may be varied according to the requirements of the designer. A very domed hammer face will produce a markedly dimpled surface. One English designer uses hammers with textured faces, and there is obviously room for experiment in this direction. Before embarking on the texturing of a form by hammering, you would be well advised to undertake trial experiments, because textured, ridged, or domed hammers will stretch the metal more than a conventional planishing hammer, and you must allow for this during the forming process. The designer must also give careful consideration to the visual effect of the texture. Should it be balanced against areas of smooth metal in order to emphasise its impact? What should be the proportion of texture to smooth surface? Elongated texture marks may enhance an elongated form, but on the other hand the designer may have reason to put horizontal textures on a tall form. Radial textures can enhance flat or shallow forms.

Finally, planishing marks may be removed completely because the designer has produced a form which does not need a busy surface. Planish the form finely and then smooth it by filing, with abrasive paper, cloth, or stone, or with a quick-cutting polishing mop and compound.

10 Wire and Tube

Wires are essential to silversmiths and jewellers in three basic ways. First of all a wire can be used in a purely practical way – as a strengthening agent in the top of a box, or teapot or in forming the bezel that holds a lid in place. In jewelry a wire may be used to strengthen the rim of a hollow sheet bracelet, or to form the skeleton or chassis on which a decorated ring or bracelet can be built up from many short lengths of wire.

Secondly, the wire may be used to fulfill a practical function, while at the same time being visible and becoming an essential part of the appearance of the finished object. For instance, a wire may be used to make the base of a dish, and its shape and width will significantly affect the appearance of the finished dish. A wire around the rim of the same dish may make it stronger and easier to pick up, but if it is set at an angle, and varies in width, its rhythms and light-catching qualities can enhance the appearance of the dish.

Finally, wires can be used as the main constituents of a design, or part of a design, in a purely creative and decorative sense. This use of wires can be found in all types of jewelry, and also in decorative pieces of holloware, such as stud boxes.

Gold, silver, copper, gilding metal, and nickel silver may all be used, and most can be obtained in round, square, and rectangular sections and in a wide range of sizes. Stainless steel can be used in wire structures, but it must be obtained in the correct dimensions because it is far too hard to reduce in draw-plates and rollers.

The tools used in manipulating wire are very modest and should include a set of pliers comprising the round-nose, square-nose, and snipe-nose varieties. Blocks of hardwood, in which slots may be cut, are invaluable, while horn and boxwood mallets may be used for trueing wire rings. Metal bars of various sections and diameters are also very useful. Cotter pins are handy for retaining wires in position during soldering. For reducing wires in size, changing their section, or making tubing, a set of draw-plates and hand draw-tongs are useful; and a busy and prosperous workshop must have a draw-bench and a set of rollers.

First of all I will describe a few basic forming techniques with wire that may be applied to any of the three categories of wire work. Bending a piece of round wire for a ring, or a flat strip for a bezel wire is simple. Just calculate the length of wire that you require, select a clean metal bar whose diameter is slightly less than the inside diameter of the ring, put the bar in a vice, and mallet each end of the wire in turn to the required curve (fig. 72). Bend the centre of the wire by hand around the bar, using the

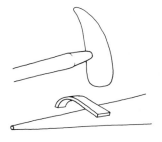

Fig. 72   Malleting a ring with a horn mallet

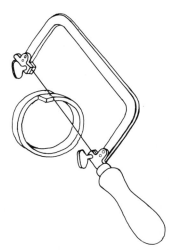

Fig. 73   Sawing the joint of a ring

Fig. 74   Closing up the joint of a ring

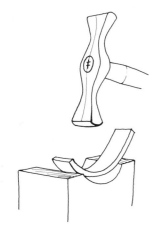

Fig. 75   Shaping a ring from thick wire

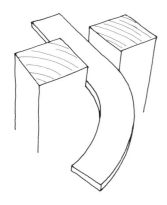

Fig. 76   Bending a flat wire in a wood block

mallet only if necessary. If you have cut too much metal, overlap the ends (fig. 73), and saw through the overlap. This will give you a joint that requires the minimum of filing. It is not necessary to make the ring absolutely circular before soldering, but it is necessary to make the joint flow reasonably and without a kink. It is almost impossible, when using thick metal, to make a small ring remotely circular, and to close the ends together it is often necessary to rest the ring joint uppermost on the bench (fig. 74), and hammer down onto each end in turn. This will result in quite a flat section at the joint, but malleting on a triblet after soldering will quickly achieve a circular form. An effective way of shaping hard or thick metal into a ring involves hammering it into a semicircular groove cut into a piece of hardwood (fig. 75). Shape each end of the metal first, using a collet hammer, and when the joint has closed up too much for hammering, revert to malleting the ends together on the bench. When soldering wire rings it is not absolutely necessary to use iron binding wire. Lay the ring flat on the hearth, and heat opposite the joint until a red heat is attained, after which the heat must be worked around to the joint, moving the flame from side to side so that both sides of the joint become equally hot. Use hard solder, which may be applied before heating as a paillon, or use a strip held in tongs.

Designs often require a ring to be made from flat wire or strip to form a ring which resembles a disc with the centre cut out. You must not attempt to make this ring by malleting the wire around a metal bar because the metal is strong in this section and it will collapse sideways under hammer blows, damaging its edge and hurting your hand with its backlash. Instead, cut a slot the same width as the wire in the end grain of a piece of hardwood plank (fig. 76). Hold the wood in a vice, slot uppermost. Place one end of the wire, with the flat section horizontal, into the slot and apply sideways pressure. The wire will bend slightly, and then begin to buckle. Move the wire further into the slot and repeat the side pressure until the metal bends again. Repeat the action until half the wire has been bent into a curve. Now start at the other end of the wire and work back into the centre. The wire will now be bent all along its length, but slightly buckled. Mallet it on a clean, flat surface, anneal it and continue bending it until the complete ring is made. It is advisable to bend a longer piece of metal than you need because it is very difficult to bend the extreme ends of the wire at all. Bend the ring and overlap the ends, cutting through the wire with a saw exactly in the centre of the overlap. True the ends with a file, and solder as described above. To true any ring finally, mallet it on a close-fitting bar or a tapered triblet, then mallet it on a flat plate to correct any warping in the other dimension. Continue this treatment until a perfectly circular and true form has been achieved.

It is often necessary to put a thickening wire into a rectangular box and lid, often to be followed by a bezel wire in the box alone. A thickening wire is usually rectangular, approximately $1·6 \times 3·175$ mm ($0·062 \times 0·125$ in.), while a bezel wire will measure $1·6 \times 6·35$ mm ($0·062 \times 0·25$ in.). You might imagine that it is best to calculate the total length of wire and bend it in three places, using the joint as the fourth corner. In fact this is far too exacting a task, and even one bend in the wrong place will make

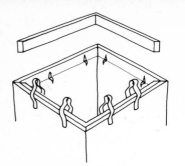

Fig. 77 Thickening wire filed and fitted, ready to be dropped into a box to rest on stitches. Half the wire is already in place, held with cotter pins

Fig. 78 Cutting a stitch with an engraving tool

the wire impossible to fit. Instead, cut two lengths of wire, and bend them in the middle, using a triangular or square file to cut the joint – as explained in Chapter 6. Fit one wire into the box, and mitre the ends, and then fit the other wire while the first is held in position with small clamps or cotter pins (fig. 77). When you solder thickening wires into boxes, vases, or any other body, you must prevent the wires slipping out of position, and falling downwards. The routine is rigid but simple. First of all clean the joint surface on the inside of the article that is to be soldered. Now scribe a line as far from the edge as the width of the wire, and with an engraving tool (fig. 78) make a short, deep cut from the edge to the scribed line. The displaced metal from the cut is pushed in front of the tool and remains projecting exactly on the scribed line. This action is called cutting a stitch. If several such stitches are cut to the scribed line, they will support the thickening wire while it is soldered into the utensil. In the case of the two pieces of thickening wire being soldered into a rectangular box, the mitred ends hold the wire tight against the box sides, while the stitches stop them from falling below the level of the top. In the case of a bezel wire the stitches must be cut on the outside surface of the bezel itself before it is lowered into the box when they will arrest its progress (fig. 79). When soldering wires into a box remember to preheat the hearth, and keep the flame low. If you get the wires red hot before the box, they will expand, buckle and warp, and you will have to take them out and true them up before trying to solder them again. Cotter pins at 1 cm (0·39 in.) intervals around the box will help to ensure a good solder joint. Lids rarely fit immediately after the soldering of wires and bezels, but have patience, if you have worked accurately, the result of cleaning off surplus solder, followed by stoning and polishing, will be a close, but easy, fit. Fig. 80 shows, in section form, variations of lid fittings and wire thicknesses.

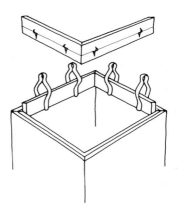

Fig. 79 Wire bezel for a box filed and stitched and ready to be dropped into place. Half the bezel is already in place, held with cotter pins

Flat wires or strips are used in miniature when making cabochon settings for stones, cameos, and sometimes ceramic plaques. The structure may consist merely of a disc of flat metal with a rim or bezel to hold the stone (fig. 81). In this case make the bezel to fit the stone, and then solder it to an over-size disc, trimming the metal later. It will be safer for the beginner to cut minute paillons of solder and place them around the bezel, after lightly wiring the structure at several points. Often, however, a back plate is not used, especially with expensive materials like gold. Instead, a bezel is made to fit the stone; a square or flat wire is shaped to fit closely inside the bezel and then soldered flush with one edge (fig. 82). The stone will

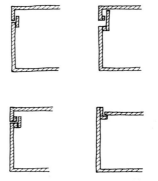

Fig. 80 Sections of various box designs, involving different wire arrangements

48

Fig. 81 Cabochon setting with solid base

Fig. 82 Cabochon setting with wire base

Fig. 83   Superb example of raising.
Jug designed by Henning Koppel and
made by Georg Jensen, Copenhagen,
Denmark

Fig. 84   Shallow dish made by sinking.
Designed by Keith Smith

Fig. 85 A typical seamed design, this pen nib was designed by Tom Scott as an annual award to the winner of a competition to find the most efficient secretary

Fig. 86 Candle construction of bent silver sheet and silver rod with a base of black nylon. Designed by Keith Smith

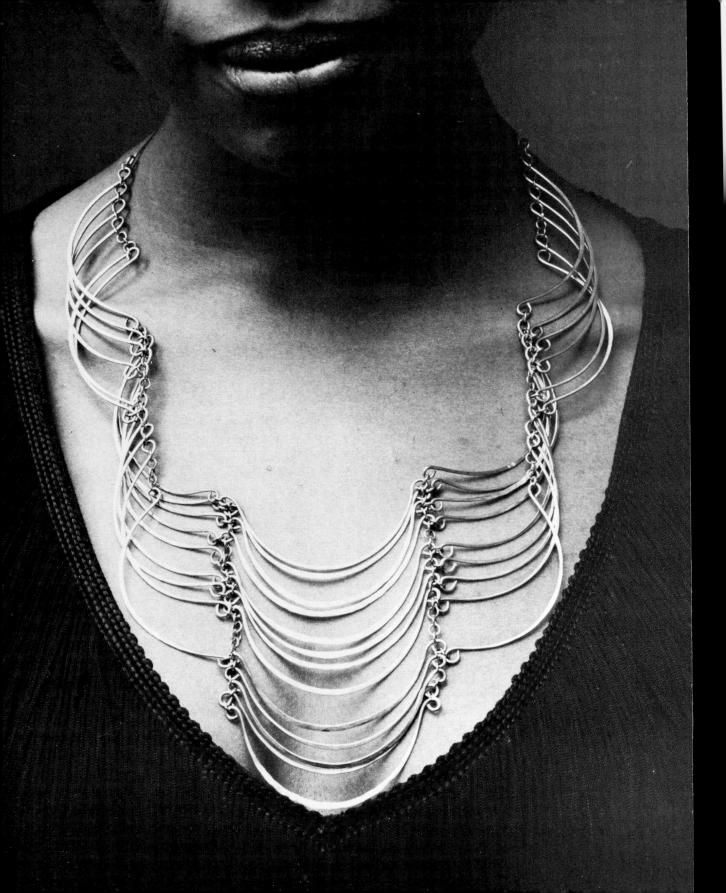

Fig. 87 Hammered steel wire necklace designed by Lesley Barlow

Fig. 88 Tall coffee pot designed by Keith Redfern

Fig. 89 Centrepiece of silver and 18-carat gold set with sapphires. Designed by Gerald Benney

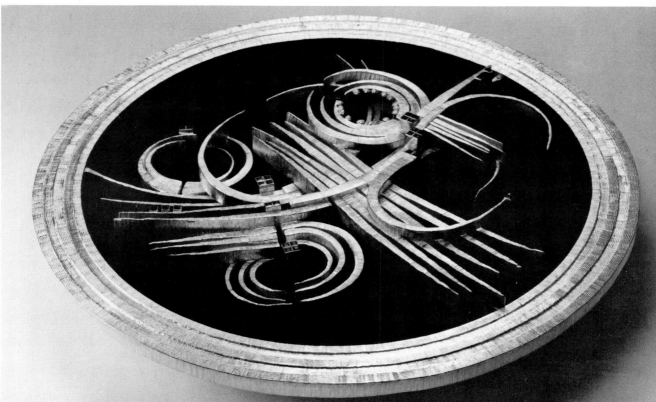

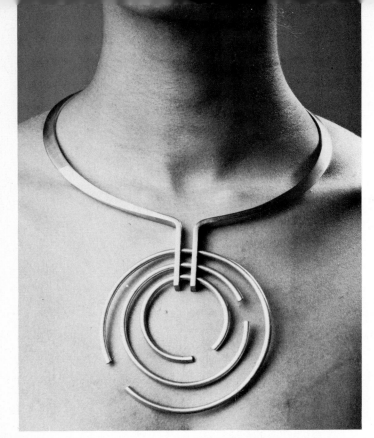

Fig. 90 Forged stainless steel necklace designed by Keith Smith

Fig. 91 Water jugs designed by Desmond Clen-Murphy. You can see the planishing marks quite clearly

Fig. 92 Three circular, textured stud boxes designed by Christopher Lawrence

Fig. 93   Crocheted stainless steel cap
designed by Georgina Thomas.
Stainless steel choker was made using
a corn dolly weaving technique;
designed by John Baldwin

Fig. 94   Chain mail and solid steel
necklace decorated with a welding
torch; designed by Douglas Wagstaff

Fig. 95 Wire work gold rings designed by William Walker

Fig. 96 Gold statuette of a bee on a honeycombe, cast from life. Designed by Leslie Durbin

Fig. 97 Stud box designed by Keith Smith. The decoration, made from square wires, was inspired by a rotted tree stump

Fig. 98   Loving cup designed by
Keith Smith. The stem was made
lost wax casting

Fig. 99   Condiment set designed
Gerald Whiles

Fig. 101   Wine cups designed by
Atholl Hill

Fig. 100   Silver box engraved all over
its visible surfaces by Malcolm
Appleby

Fig. 102   Five-a-side
football trophy
designed by
Keith Smith

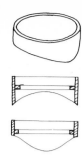

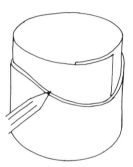

Fig. 103 Cabochon setting shaped to fit closely to the fingers

then rest on the wire. If the setting is for a ring, and is wide, it may need the lower edge shaped to match the curve of the finger. In this case a deep bezel and a deep inner wire will be needed to allow metal to be filed away to fit the finger (fig. 103), and yet provide a level shelf for the stone. Cameos rarely sit on a regular level – the perimeter rises and falls – and in this case the bezel must once again be made rather deep, as must the inside wire which must be filed to accommodate the cameo levels. Before setting a cameo, you will have to adjust the top edge of the bezel to correspond with the level of the cameo.

In discussing irregular levels in wires it is worth noting the problems of thickening the edge of a vessel which has a top profile that rises and falls. The vessel must be carefully shaped before the wire is made; if it has the appropriate profile it can be inverted and rubbed over emery cloth that is wrapped tightly around a bar and held in a vice. A tube of stiff paper must now be inserted into the mouth of the vessel and allowed to spring open so that it presses all round the inner surface. Hold the paper in place and draw a line on it by tracing around the lip of the vessel (fig. 104).

Fig. 104 Paper tube should be marked with a pencil to produce the development for a thickening wire

Fig. 105 Paper from fig. 104 opened flat to show development of top edge

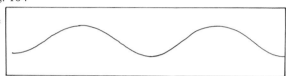

Take the paper out and lay it on the bench (fig. 105). The wavy line represents the development of the thickening wire. Use a wood block, as already described, to bend a flat wire to match the drawing (fig. 106). Now turn it to a circle around a bar and the thickening wire is complete (fig. 107). After soldering it may require some trueing with a mallet. This method can be used for any vessel.

As already suggested, wires may be used as a chassis on which to construct rings and bracelets or necklaces where the surface is built up of many separate pieces of metal such as discs or domes, pieces of sheet, or a network of wires. The purpose of the chassis is to support the form but it may also provide the necessary comfortable fitting surfaces of a ring or bracelet. It is usual to use a minimum of two wires, one at each edge of the object, but it is also often necessary to solder lateral wires to join the perimeter wires, and perhaps to shape them to set the contours of the object. Though the chassis may be mainly covered on the finished object, if it is to be visible at all it must be designed as an integral part of the structure.

Fig. 106 Flat thickening wire is bent in wood block

Fig. 107 Thickening wire in place in the body

Making and soldering perimeter wires for a bracelet or ring chassis uses techniques already described, but joining them together requires additional guidance, and confidence and initiative are needed for this sort of project. Some jewellers use fireproof putty to support joints while they are being soldered; others use spring tweezers to hold one component at a right

Fig. 108 Ring showing chassis with cabochon setting acting as a spacer and tie at the top, and some of decorative surface in place lower down

angle, while the other lies on the hearth; and yet others make little metal jigs, or just prop up components with small pieces of hearth brick. Often the angle of a joint can be altered very slightly by using pliers. Very often a design requires a narrow width in one or more places and this is always the best place to make the first joint. Once the perimeter wires are joined in one place, you may be able to begin building the decorative surface as far away from that place as possible. The structure is very soon extremely strong, and if you keep your flame small previous joints need not be melted. The use of solders with various melting points is also of help in these cases. The technique of applying solder is important in this type of project, and a variety of methods may be employed according to personal experience and preference. The time-honoured method of putting the components together and placing paillons in position before heating is safe and effective, but as experience grows you may prefer to heat the components and apply paillons with tweezers just before the melting point of the solders is reached. It is possible to apply a tiny stick of solder to the joint, although it is very easy to flood a joint in this way.

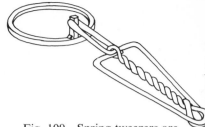

Fig. 109 Spring tweezers are used to hold a vertical wire steady before soldering. Note small piece of solder at joint

A design made up from wires soldered together into a pattern spread over a flat surface is easily constructed by simply laying the elements next to each other on the hearth (fig. 110). Heating must proceed with caution because the flux may displace and push apart the wires, and they may need adjusting with tweezers as the flux runs. For this reason it may be necessary to solder only a few components at a time, gradually building the final object.

I would like to draw your attention to a use of wire which is more like textile working. Most wires can be formed into jewelry forms by weaving, macramé knotting, French knitting, through a bobbin, and by corn dolly techniques. These are attractive techniques and have much to offer to anyone who wishes to enter a rather more unusual field in metal forming.

Fig. 110 Strips of wire to form decoration or jewelry are laid in place prior to soldering. Note small pieces of solder at each joint

Wires and tube may also be used to make decoration by soldering short lengths side by side and displaying them vertically so that the cross sections make up the pattern. This type of decoration may also be used when the lengths of wire or tube are soldered to a back plate, leaving space between each piece of material. It is a technique suitable for both jewelry and holloware and can be soldered by fluxing the back plate, arranging the wires on it, and sprinkling fine paillons of solder all over the surface. Slowly heat the work so as not to cause the wires to move unduly, or to fall over, and increase the heat until the solder runs. In designing this form of decoration you must bear in mind that there is bound to be some movement of the wires, and the technique does not lend itself to patterns of extreme geometric accuracy. Tube can also be used to build all manner of decoration, and if the ends are cut diagonally to show elliptical holes, intriguing qualities can be developed. Tube can also be bent, though only a little at a time, and then only when it is filled with resin to prevent it kinking or flattening. Plug one end of the tube, fill it with powdered resin, packing it tight, and then apply heat. The resin will melt and shrink and more powder must be added until the tube is full. The tube can then be carefully bent around any suitable object using hand pressure. Annealing may be necessary in which case the resin must be burnt out and then

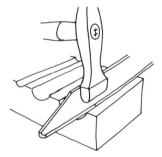

Fig. 111 Tube blank hammered into a metal swage block. Note point on the end of the blank

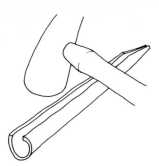

Fig. 112 Tube blank malleted on the bench to form a rough tube before it is pulled through a draw-plate

Fig. 113 Tube can be pulled through a draw-plate and reduced in size.

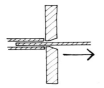

Fig. 114 Wire core pulled out of a piece of tube

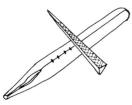

Fig. 115 Mark the line of the joint on a finished tube with a triangular needle file

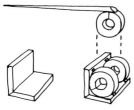

Fig. 116 Components of a brooch hinge

replaced. It is a slow business but it enables you to achieve some fine qualities. Tube can be purchased in a variety of sizes and wall thicknesses, but it can also be made from sheet metal with the aid of a swage block or a block of hardwood in which channels can be cut, a collet hammer, and draw-plates and a draw-bench.

The width of the blank of metal from which the tube will be made is calculated by multiplying the tube diameter by $\frac{22}{7}$. The blank should be at least as long as the tube will need to be, plus 2 or 3 cm (about 1 in.) to allow a point to be cut at one end. Anneal the blank, place it over the widest groove in the swage block, and hammer all along its length (fig. 111), sinking it to a gutter section. If possible work into the narrower grooves until the hammer will no longer fit, or the width of the shaped metal is the same as that of the required tube. Now lay the metal on the bench with both edges uppermost, and tap along each edge in turn (fig. 112). This will turn the edges over and towards each other until they close up. The ends of the blank will tend to curl up, but can be straightened by hand. The tube section will be far from round at this stage, but the draw-plate will soon correct that. Draw-plates have tapered holes, and you will discover which hole will start to true the tube by putting the pointed end through the wider side of a hole that is obviously too large. Now try the next smallest hole until you come to one that only the point of the tube will penetrate. If you then pull the tube through the hole it will be reduced in diameter (fig. 113) as it passes down the taper, and it will become slightly longer. It can now be drawn through four or five more holes before annealing is necessary. The tube must always be oiled or greased first. If, as you reduce the tube in size, the inside diameter becomes too small, or the wall of the tube too thick, you must insert a greased steel wire, and continue drawing the tube with the wire in place. The tube will grow longer, creeping along the wire, which must be long enough to allow for this. The wire must be removed before each annealing. To do this push the projecting end of the steel wire through the narrow side of a draw-plate hole that is smaller than the tube (fig. 114), and pull it out. The tube has a seam, of course, and if it is to be used for a hinge it need not be soldered; otherwise solder it as soon as it is round and the joint is closed up tightly. If it is not to be soldered, mark the joint with file nicks (fig. 115) so that you can find it easily.

Hinges represent an important use of tubing and are needed in boxes, bracelets, collars, and brooches. The simplest form of tube hinge is to be found in a brooch where the pin has to be fitted to the back of the piece of jewelry. It consists simply of a piece of sheet bent to a right angle, with the pieces of tube soldered into the angle (fig. 116) with a gap between them for the tube on the end of the brooch pin to be inserted and held in place by a hard rivet pin. One side of the angled sheet is soldered to the back of the brooch and the other faces inwards towards the brooch catch. As the pin is lowered it is checked by the edge of the angled sheet and has to be sprung into the brooch catch, making the brooch much more secure when worn. The sheet can be made simply by bending with pliers, or more professionally, by filing a V and then bending it. The tube can now be cut. First of all true the end of the tube with a fine file, then cut a piece off;

true the end again and cut the second piece off. Balance your bent sheet, point downwards, in the rib of a hearth brick, or in a groove in a carbon block, lightly flux the inside faces of the angle and the V joint, and place the two pieces of the tube making sure that the seams are turned into the soldering area, and that the rough sawn sides face outwards. Place a very small paillon of solder on either side of each piece of tube (see fig. 116), warm the whole structure slowly so that the flux does not displace the tubes, and finally increase the heat until the solder runs. Pickle the hinge and file each side smooth.

A hinge for a box, bracelet, or coffee pot is rather more difficult. The point at which the hinge is made must have sufficient thickness of metal in which to embed the segments or knuckles of tube which interlock to form the hinge. In the case of a straight-sided box it is necessary to solder into one side of the box a wire 3 mm (0·125 in.) square. A similar wire must be soldered into the matching side of the lid. The tube from which the hinge is to be formed should be approximately 3 mm (0·125 in.) in diameter, and if it is to be seamed mark the join with nicks all along its length. Roll the tube between metal flat plates to make sure it is straight. Now file a small chamfer along the edge of the box on the side in which the wire is soldered, and carry out a similar operation on the lid (fig. 117).

Place the lid on the box with the chamfers face to face and tape the box and lid tightly together. It is now necessary to deepen with a file or scraper the chamfer at the joint of the lid and the box until you have made a groove which will hold the hinge tube tightly. This can be done with a round-edge joint file (fig. 119), that is a flat file with teeth only on rounded edges, the flat faces being quite smooth. If such a file is used the groove must be checked constantly because you may remove more metal at each end, making it both wider and deeper. If you complete such a hinge it will be curved and will not work properly, and it will be sloppy with large gaps at each end. Careful filing with locked wrists will help to eliminate this problem. However, it is usually necessary to work on the centre of the groove at some time during the process, and to do this you should work with the tip of the file, making sure not to file the ends at all. Check the trueness of the groove with a straight edge. It is also possible to cut the groove with a scraper made from an old square file (fig. 120). The end should be bent over and shaped so that it will scrape a semicircular groove in the box. Steady scraping, first in one direction, and then the other, will achieve the same effect as a round-edge joint file.

Most hinges allow a lid to open to a right angle and no more, and to achieve this, the tube must be sunk into the bearer three quarters of its diameter. This means that you must cut a groove of the correct depth in the box and lid, but it should only be half as wide as the tube. Now separate the box and lid (fig. 121) and widen the groove in each until, when lid and box are put together again, the gap at the surface is still the same width, but the groove has been shaped enough to allow the hinge tube to be pushed in from either end without forcing box and lid apart.

You must now decide how many pieces of tube or 'knuckles' are needed for your box, remembering that it should always be an odd number, which means, for instance, three on the lid and four on the box – always more on

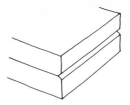

Fig. 117   Box with chamfers or bevels cut prior to cutting a round groove to take the hinge

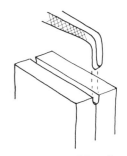

Fig. 118   Box with a deep, round-bottomed groove cut with a tool made from an old file or a round-edge joint file

Fig. 119   Round-edge file

Fig. 120   Scraper made from an old file

Fig. 121   Half box showing bezel and hinge groove cut to shape

Fig. 122 A chamfer on each knuckle will give the correct joint with the bearer or hinge groove

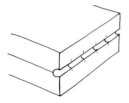

Fig. 123 Hinge groove marked out to show how long each hinge knuckle should be

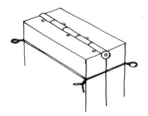

Fig. 124 Box wired for soldering, with solder pieces in position

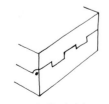

Fig. 125 A flush hinge

the box. Should you decide upon only three knuckles between box and lid, make the one on the lid longer than the two on the box. Cut the tubes slightly over length and carefully true the end faces so that each will fit tightly up to the next. Use a special joint tool and a file, hold the tube in a miniature lathe and use a file, or simply twist the tube between finger and thumb while holding it vertical against the bench pin and file across the end as it revolves backwards and forwards. With a file, slightly chamfer each end of the knuckles for one third of the circumference, equally on either side of the seam, if there is one (fig. 122). Assemble the box, push the knuckles into place and then, with a pencil, mark the lid and the box where each knuckle meets the next. Draw lines across the groove with a pencil to mark the divisions between the knuckles (fig. 123). With the pencil shade those areas of the groove on the box and the lid which will not have hinge tube soldered to them, and lightly borax those areas which will be soldered. Pencil the ends of each hinge knuckle and place each one in the groove on the box, placing the seam into the borax for the box knuckles, and facing the seam upwards for the lid knuckles, so that they will be embedded in the boraxed areas on the lid. Now paint rouge on all fitting parts of the box, lower the lid into position, and wire the box together, making sure that there are loops at each corner so as not to damage the edges of the box. Place the box on the hearth, hinge uppermost. Cut small paillons of solder and place one centrally on the box side of each box knuckle, and one centrally on the lid side of each lid knuckle (fig. 124). Slowly heat the whole box, keeping the flame from the knuckles because they will tend to get hot too quickly. Aim to reach soldering heat for the lid, box, and knuckles at the same time, and as soon as the solder melts stop heating. Remove the binding wire and leave the box to cool – do not pickle it. When it is cool open it, lay box and lid separately on the hearth, and add as little solder as possible, in the form of paillons, to solder the knuckles securely in place without flooding the joints and preventing a proper fit between box and lid. At no stage during the soldering of a hinge should a stick of solder be used – it invites disaster. Too much solder can result in the classic silversmith's joke – a lid soldered to its box. The pencilling of non-soldering surfaces helps to stop solder running amok if too much is applied, while the chamfers on the hinge tubes do the same thing, and stop fillets forming at the joint of tube endings and causing the lid and box not to fit properly. If a thick-walled tube is used for the hinge, the part that projects at the back of the box can be filed off to give a flush surface to the hinge (fig. 125). (Pencilling on rouge refers to brushing on of yellow ochre or other substance to retard the flow of heat (U.S.).)

The principles described above can be applied to any hinge on any object, from bracelets to coffee pots, but intelligent adaptation has to be made according to individual circumstances. A hinge on a cylindrical body must be either very short, or cut very deeply. In any case, the hinge has to be straight and will therefore project at the ends, the outer knuckles not being sunk deeply, and not having much metal to solder onto. Alternatively, the hinge can be soldered onto the outside of the body, though this needs careful designing so that the hinge does not look like an afterthought. The appearance of any hinge must be considered very carefully.

11 Decoration

Surface decoration stamps the personality of a designer upon his or her work. The problem for many beginners is to decide how to translate an idea on paper or in the mind into metal. This chapter sets out a variety of techniques you can easily experiment with, so that you can build up a dictionary of decoration technique.

Stamping or punching

This is a simple technique. Suitable metals include, silver, gold, copper, gilding metal, and in certain cases stainless steel. Punches are best made from tool steel, though for soft metals a punch made from less hard material may be adequate. Basically there are two types of punch mark. There is the sort which has a precise, incised quality and leaves the metal relatively undistorted, and there is the soft-edged, deep punch mark which contours the surface of the form and sets up a very reflective surface.

The first category of punching is carried out with a flat-faced punch with sharp edges. The punch must not be too large in its stamping face, otherwise it will meet too much resistance to penetrate the surface of the metal, will tend to bounce, and will leave an unwanted double image. The face of the punch may take any form, from long and narrow to square, triangular, round or oval. Its face may be highly polished or textured. A textured punch mark can look most effective on a highly polished metal surface. The face of the punch need only be left with a file finish to attain this result. The punching is actually carried out by placing the work on a good metal surface, putting the punch in position, and striking it firmly with a hammer. It is worth trying the punch on a piece of scrap metal first, just to get the feel of the action. This type of punching can be used to produce an abstract texture of a random or regular quality. Regular punching can be arranged in radial patterns, or half-drop rectilinear patterns or indeed any arrangement which enhances a form. Alternatively, it can be used to produce a stylized representation of natural form, or any other idea derived from the source of reference which interests or intrigues you. Only a good deal of thought, observation, drawing and experimenting will give you the best results in this type of work. It is simply no use picking up a punch with a pleasant shape, starting to decorate at one side, and hoping that it will all come right. Quite obviously you are not restricted to the use of one punch on one object, and of course punching can be combined with pierced holes or applied wires. Punching should always be carried out on a surface that has already been finished, as excessive cleaning

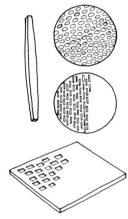

Fig. 126 Sharp-edged punch, and some simple variations of pattern

Fig. 127 Deep-contour punch and the pattern it produces

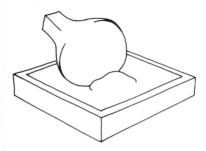

Fig. 128   Hot pitch should be moved with a large, cold, metal stake

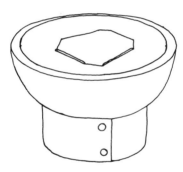

Fig. 129   Pitch bowl and collar containing a flat blank. The corners are turned down and embedded in pitch

Fig. 130   Flat blank with corners turned down to hold it in the pitch

of a punched surface is bound to destroy essential qualities. In conclusion this is a technique very suitable for the beginner because random and less exacting decoration can look good, but it may well continue to appeal to a designer as skill and discrimination develop.

Deep-contour punching is carried out on a metal surface which has a cushion of softer metal under it, such as sheet lead. Alternatively, the object can be filled with pitch or set on a pitch tray. You can discover the effect of deep punching stage by stage. First polish your metal, and then punch it with a fairly heavy blow of the hammer. The punch will print its form in the metal, but will also sink in some distance to give a reflective contour around it. Punch another mark some distance away, and another until you have covered the surface. The contours around the punch marks will run into each other and interact on each other and the surface will be criss-crossed with reflections. Any shape of punch can be used for this technique and the punch pattern should be related in scale and arrangement to the form which it covers.

Chasing and repoussé

The use of punches leads us naturally to consider the technique of chasing and repoussé which is currently enjoying a revival. Chasing can be exploited to produce a simple line decoration which can be varied in emphasis by deepening or widening the line. It has a completely different character to engraving, which is more crisp and sensitive. Repoussé is the art of embossing the metal from the back, and is usually carried out on metal that has been line-chased on the front side to define the limits of the contours.

Both techniques are carried out on metal that has been set into pitch. The pitch is contained in either a shallow box (fig. 128), or a bowl which rests in a leather collar (fig. 129) which allows the bowl and the work to be tilted in any direction for easy working. The pitch can be bought from a silversmiths' or jewellers' suppliers, and is often called Swedish pitch. It must be melted with a gentle heat and have resin, tallow, and plaster of Paris added to it, because pitch by itself is too brittle. The essential quality of this mixture is that it will give where the metal is pushed down, while it supports the surrounding metal. A suitable recipe consists of 6 parts pitch, 8 parts plaster, 1 part resin, and 1 part linseed oil. Pitch should always be heated gently, particularly if a gas torch is passed over the surface, because it will harden if burnt. Your metal must be annealed before it is fixed to the pitch, and in the case of repoussé work it must be removed at intervals for more annealing or it will break down.

A design on a flat piece of metal is worked on a blank that is appreciably larger than the design itself, otherwise as you chase near the edge of the design, the metal will buckle and distort. Some craftsmen cut a rectangular blank and bend the corners downwards (fig. 130) so that the metal is held even more firmly. Heat the surface of the pitch gently, and press your metal onto it. It is sometimes a good idea to push the hot pitch into a mound with a large, cold metal stake, so that when a piece of flat metal is placed centrally on it and pressed downwards, the pitch spreads outwards,

71

eliminating all air pockets. If you find that the metal sounds hollow and subsides as you work it, it has an air pocket underneath and must be removed and reset. A bowl or hollowed shape that has to be chased on its convex face must be filled with pitch before you set it in the pitch bowl. The pitch can be put into the object in lumps and melted with a torch, or poured from a heated pan.

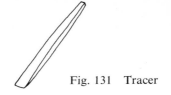

Fig. 131   Tracer

A line-chasing tool, or tracer, resembles a miniature cold chisel (fig. 131), though the working end is polished and rounded and should not cut the metal at all. Hold the tool between the first three fingers and the thumb, with the third finger right at the bottom of the tool, by the working edge, so that it can brush the metal as you chase. Place the tool on the metal at some point on the drawn design and strike it gently but rapidly with a chasing hammer, as you move it slowly along the design, preferably working towards yourself. The metal will be pushed down into the pitch, making a corresponding ridge on its underside. The line may be deepened or widened by heavier hammering or changing to a blunter-edged tool. Long, straight lines are best chased with a wide or long-edged tool, sharply curved lines with a narrow one. Many beginners find it difficult to chase a smooth line and produce instead a dotted and jerky one. Smooth, slow, movements of the tool and light but fast tapping with the hammer should help to give a good result. If the tool deviates from the required line, start again beyond it and work back past the mistake. You must always use a chasing hammer which has a slender, whippy handle shaft (fig. 133) which widens out into a bulb-shaped end to fit the palm of the hand. It has a wide, flat-faced head with which to tap the tool, and a ball pein opposite, for hollowing metal. Holloware can be chased by filling the body with pitch and setting a stick into it, so that it projects enough to be held in the vice while you work.

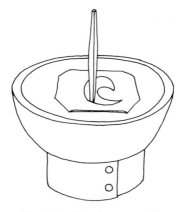

Fig. 132   Tracing an outline

Fig. 133   Chasing hammer

If a piece is to be embossed you must line-chase the limits of the contours first, turn the metal over, reset it on the pitch and work from the back. The limits of the design will be defined by a ridge, and the metal can be punched to the required contour using a rounded punch that is tapped over the surface using sweeping movements to follow the contours. The metal will get hard and may need annealing before the final shape is attained. If you require sharp ridges, do not attempt to sharpen them too soon, and be prepared to use a tracer or sharp-edged tool if necessary. You may need to emboss areas on embossed forms, in which case you will need to line-chase on the already embossed area, before punching the next level. If the repoussé work has to be carried out on a flat blank of metal, it will always warp, even if the corners are turned down to help hold it flat in the pitch. When this happens, take the metal off the pitch, place it on a flat plate, and punch all around the edge of the embossing with a hard-wood punch (fig. 134). This should be done at any time when annealing is necessary.

Fig. 134   Flatten a warped blank with a wood punch

When you wish to anneal the metal warm it gently, lift it off the pitch with tongs, continue to warm it gently until as much pitch as possible has run off, and then heat it vigorously, burning the pitch residue until the coke glows with bright spots. When you remove the flame the spots will be grey-white, and if the metal is instantly quenched and then pickled,

72

most pitch traces should vanish, and the remainder can be removed by scrubbing with pumice powder and water.

Having embossed the metal slightly more than you need, anneal it and reset it with the outer surface uppermost. The metal now requires planishing and generally refining because it will appear rather bumpy. You can use any tool that will do the job without cutting or damaging the surface. An oval punch with a gently curved face, sometimes called a pearl (fig. 135), is a good general-purpose planisher. Chase with flowing movements over the contours, and the bumps and hollows will vanish and be replaced with miniature planishing marks. Square-faced tools, or tools with angled, flat faces can be used to sharpen corners and edges. The beginner may find this difficult and may even have to fall back on a fine file and a water of Ayr stone to tidy the metal surface. The most common fault is heavy, impatient hammering that results in holes in the work. You must work slowly and systematically.

Fig. 135   Planishing tool

Etching

This is an interesting method of decoration, which requires no skilled metalwork technique. Basically, metal is coated with an acid-resistant varnish or ground and the design is scratched and scraped away, to reveal the metal underneath. It is then immersed in an etchant – an acid or other corrosive liquid – and the bare metal will be eaten away to reveal an incised decoration when the varnish is removed. The technique is suitable for most metals, even stainless steel, although it etches very slowly.

Etching ground can be obtained from specialist suppliers in liquid form for easy application with a soft brush. The metal should be cleaned well and de-greased before you apply the ground. It must be applied to all surfaces. Coat the metal with firm strokes of the brush and do not coat it too thickly. Thick ground tends to be brittle and cracks very easily during the etching process. When the ground is dry, the design may be scratched and scraped onto the surface with a fine needle. A worn needle file, sharpened to a point, will do the job well. Acids must be mixed for use, remember that they are very dangerous, and that acid must always be added to water. Acid can be used in a heatproof glass dish, and should always be used in a fuming cupboard or a well ventilated place. Home craftsmen should keep acid under lock and key. Silver can be etched with a solution of 2 parts water, and 1 part nitric acid. For copper and gilding metal use 1 part of water to 1 part acid, or alternatively perchloride of iron and water.

Place the metal which is to be etched into acid so that it is covered by about 1 cm (0·4 in.). Bubbles of gas will form and rise to the surface as the etchant begins to work. Rock the dish to help clear the bubbles, or wipe them off with a feather. It is better to etch slowly with a diluted etchant rather than use a concentrated solution which will quickly etch sideways as well as downwards and will cause the ground to lift off the metal. When the metal has been in the acid for some time feel the depth of the etched area with a needle, and when you think that you have achieved the necessary depth remove the work from the acid, using tongs. Wash it and examine it. At this stage you should decide whether to deepen some parts of the design; depth variation can add a great deal of interest and subtlety to a design. You can do this by painting ground onto those parts of the design which are already deep enough, and leaving bare those parts which are to be etched to a greater depth.

Although etching is in many ways a comparatively easy technique, things can still go wrong. To achieve a particular effect may require a lot of experiment and experience. Etching, like other decorative techniques, should be carried out on a finished, polished surface, because heavy cleaning and polishing will destroy subtle qualities and details.

Flame decoration

Some materials can be decorated or textured with a flame. Silver, copper, and gilding metal can be heated with intense torch flames until the surface begins to melt. The surface need not necessarily be cleaned or boraxed before heating, because a clean surface melts cleanly, whereas an oxidized surface retains a skin which ripples as the under-surface begins to melt. This technique is most easily carried out on flat sheet that can be laid on a brick, which limits the chance of sudden and total collapse of the metal. With practice and experience a fair measure of control can be achieved with this technique, but the beginner would be wise to experiment on scrap metal.

An oxyacetylene welding torch can be used to burn holes in sheet metal and the resulting effect can be intriguing because the lip of each hole has a rounded edge with small radiating ridges and ripples. The natural or accidental quality of the holes contrasts with the flat sheet between the holes, and the rounded edges catch the light when they are polished. This is a technique which is particularly effective on stainless steel, even more so if the oxide colours are allowed to remain on the finished article.

Piercing and sawing

Pierced holes made with drills or saws are another attractive form of decoration, used either alone on sheet metal, or in conjunction with chasing or applied wires, tube, or metal shot. Remember that holes can have an endless variety of interesting shapes. The metal, its thickness between the holes and the patterns traced around each hole and from hole to hole must also be considered. What happens in the space beyond the holes is also important. A sense of mystery may become as much a part of your design as all the metal which you have carefully shaped.

If holes are to be pierced in metal they may, of course, be simple drilled holes of various sizes, but holes of a large size, or a shape other than round are usually cut with a piercing saw. Transfer the design to the metal by using carbon paper, with careful free-hand drawing, or by glueing a tracing to the surface of the metal. If the design is drawn or traced onto the surface it may be better to scribe it before starting work. Drill a small hole somewhere within each area that is to be cut out, preferably nearest the outer edge of the component. In the case of a large or complex and irregular

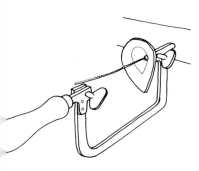

Fig. 136 Piercing saw with a blank threaded onto the blade

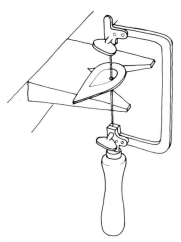

Fig. 137 Sawing a blank on a bench pin

shaped area, two or three drilled holes may be needed so that sawing can be carried out from different directions. The metal is best rested on a bench pin whilst sawing is carried out.

Piercing saws can be bought in varying frame sizes, and some have an adjustable frame so that short lengths of saw blade can be used. Saw blades can be bought in varying sizes; the finest have teeth that can hardly be seen with the naked eye. Always use a reasonably fine blade for the job; if the teeth are too far apart they will catch and jag on thin sheet metal, giving a rough edge to the saw cut. An expert piercer using the correct blade uses a file seldom, if ever, for refining his work. The teeth of a piercing saw should always point towards the handle, so that as you draw the saw downwards, the blade cuts the metal. Never force the saw, just move it up and down and it will cut; to change direction simply swing the frame. To use a saw when piercing holes put the saw blade in the top jaws of the frame and tighten the wing nut. Thread the other end of the blade through the hole in the work and slide the work up the blade to the top jaws. Press the end of the saw frame against the bench by leaning on the end of the handle and tighten the saw blade in the jaws at the handle end of the saw. Release your pressure on the saw and the frame will spring apart and stretch the blade taut. A saw blade must always be as taut as possible if it is to work properly and to last for any time at all. To begin sawing, hold your work in one hand, and the saw handle in the hand with which you will work it. Place the saw blade within the V of the bench pin and lower the work onto the pin, so that the metal is now supported on either side of the saw blade (fig. 137). Hold the metal firmly and saw steadily and gently, holding the saw in a relaxed grip. Some craftsmen wipe the blade across the palm of the hand to grease it a little, to make the saw work more easily. If you wish to turn a sharp corner, saw right up to the turning point, press very gently sideways in the direction opposite the one that you are about to follow, and with a sawing motion gradually swing the saw frame round until the blade is pointing in the right direction. The side pressure on the blade gives the teeth room to turn easily. You may find at times that with large or complex holes you need to remove the saw blade and start again from another hole.

Sheet metal

The application of wire and tube for decorative purposes has already been discussed in Chapter 10, but sheet metal can also be used for decoration. To apply metal sheet as a lamination can prove a very exacting task. If the sheet has a large surface area, it must be made to fit its base exactly. It must not rock on the surface, because gaps will be left at the edges when it is soldered, and neither must it be domed to leave hollows between the two pieces of metal. Soldering can also pose problems. If you put a decorative piece of sheet in place on its base and solder it with a stick or paillons of solder, pools of solder – and worse, burn marks – often remain at the soldering points. Attempts to tidy the marks with a file or a stone result in slight hollows in the surface of the metal which reflect light, and rounded corners which ought to have been sharp. Perhaps a better method is to melt solder onto the back of the decorative sheet first, spreading the solder with a piece of binding wire if necessary. After the metal has cooled, it can be boraxed, placed on its base and heated until the solder runs freely. In point of fact difficulties in soldering one large piece of sheet to another can easily be eliminated by cutting a hole in the piece of metal to which the sheet is to be soldered, leaving a joint of perhaps 3 mm (0·159 in.) all round the edge.

Metal shot

This looks very attractive as a decoration or element of decoration on jewelry and holloware. It is easily made by cutting small pieces of metal and melting them on a charcoal or compressed carbon block. Soldering shot onto work may be a problem because of the difference in size between the two pieces of metal. Always build the heat up slowly, and bring it onto the shot as late as possible, otherwise you are very likely to flood the shot with an unsightly fillet of solder.

12   Casting

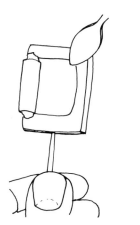

Fig. 138   Rough wax chassis constructed from wax sticks and attached to a metal rod for easy handling

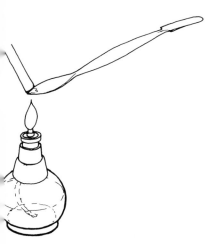

Fig. 139   Heat a steel modelling tool over a spirit lamp to melt a stick of wax onto its blade

Casting has become very popular with jewellers and silversmiths in recent years because materials and equipment are now easier to obtain, and because designer-craftsmen are more curious, more resourceful, and more adventurous in their techniques. This chapter deals with vacuum, centrifugal, steam pressure, and cuttlefish casting.

Craftsmen can practice lost wax casting with relatively simple equipment, some of which can be made quite easily. It usually involves the making of a wax model of exactly the dimension and shape the designer has conceived. The model is then embedded in investment plaster, which is left to set. The wax is burnt out of the plaster in a kiln, which is then heated to the temperature suggested by the plaster manufacturer, after which molten metal is introduced to the cavity left by the burnt wax. The casting is then broken out of the plaster and worked up to the required finish.

There are many types of wax for use by the expert or specialist. However you need only consider a few basic types for modelling. Carving wax is universally useful because it can be filed, sawn, carved, or built up with a hot modelling tool. You can buy it as a block or in slices, or you may prefer blue inlay wax which is marketed in sticks and may be more convenient to use. Both types of wax are quite hard, and do not soften or melt when held in the hand – the important qualities. You can use carving and inlay waxes to make almost any object.

Files and saws are easily obtainable, but you may have to make special modelling and carving tools. You can make a modelling tool from round steel rod 6 mm (0·236 in.) in diameter and 12 cm (4·724 in.) long. Each end should be forged to a flat blade 1·5 mm (0·051 in.) thick, and then sawn or filed to the required profiles. Finish the blades with convex faces and sharp edges. You must make the blades taper to a narrow neck before widening to a shaft that is comfortable and easy to hold. The narrow neck ensures that heat does not pass into the handle and also that the heat can be built up quickly, and lost quickly if you get the tool too hot.

Your first step in building up a form is to carve a rough blank or skeleton in wax, or to break up some lengths of stick wax and fuse them together for the same purpose. You can hold it in your hand while you build it up or, better still, spike it on an old needle file so that your fingers do not get in the way, or get burnt by hot wax. Warm the modelling tool in the flame of a bunsen burner or a spirit lamp. Home workers may be tempted to use a candle, but this is not very satisfactory because carbon is deposited on the tool which impairs the working qualities of the wax.

When the tool is warmed, spoon up a little wax from a block, or apply a stick of wax to the surface of the blade with the hand that holds the model, warm the tool a little more until the wax runs and then tilt the tool, point touching the model, and trail the wax where you want it. If the tool is too hot the wax will flood across the model in the most uncontrollable manner; if it is not hot enough, it will set as soon as it touches the model. Obviously you must learn to control the wax but this only takes an hour or two. Any contour and form can be built up by this method, and if, for instance, you dab the tool continuously in one position, blowing gently on the model at the same time, you can build up a long delicate spike. You can build a texture of wax globules on the surface of a model by blobbing one globule of wax into position at a time, though if the tool is too hot you may drown all the globules that you have already made. The clearest indications of an over-hot modelling tool are the smell of burning wax, rising smoke, and black carbon on the faces of the tool.

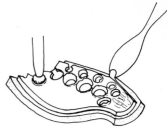

Fig. 140   Wax spread on a shaped plaster base. One edge has been built up with wax trailed from a modelling tool, and a decorative surface has been formed with a hot, round-headed punch

Experiment to discover just what wax will do for you. For example, a hot metal rod drawn across the surface of a flat sheet of wax will make a deep channel. Repeat the action to produce parallel channels, cut further channels at right angles, and cut holes at channel intersections; an intriguing surface will result. Hot punches pressed into the surface of wax may also produce rewarding qualities. You should experiment in an enquiring way, and will most certainly be driven to it at times, when after visualizing some exciting ideas, you have to work out how to produce them. Experimenting with wax for decoration is, of course, just like exploiting any other material and technique. At first you will be carried along by excitement, but you will quickly exhaust your immediate ideas and will have to get down to hard thinking and searching for sources of reference, if you are to produce any significant ideas.

Fig. 141   Plaster core for a ring with wax decoration on the top

When you have built your model to roughly the required form, you must work on the finish that you require in metal. Flat planes must be perfectly flat, edges must be sharp, and curves must be quite true. It is a waste of time and metal to achieve these qualities by filing the metal casting, not to mention the risk of uncovering air pockets beneath the surface. Also, of course, wax modelling allows you to model undercuts and concave surfaces which are most difficult to smooth and true after casting. To smooth and burnish your wax model you should slightly warm a modelling tool and with flowing, smoothing actions, pass it backwards and forwards over the surface of the wax. The convex surface of the modelling tool will minimize the risk of its edge digging into the wax, and as long as you take care to establish the correct heat for the tool, you will produce a finely burnished surface. You can also pass the model quickly through a flame, though this is not a good idea with a model that combines textures with smooth surfaces.

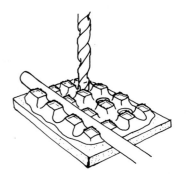

Fig. 142   Wax spread on plaster can be shaped with a hot wire or drilled

Carving and building up wax are probably the most popular techniques in use, but sheet waxes can also be exploited. Sheet wax usually becomes flexible when it is held over a flame or immersed in hot water. By pushing it around in your fingers, pleating it, and folding it, you will find that it is possible to produce all manner of forms. You can pierce holes in sheet wax by heating a wire, pushing it through the wax and quickly blowing to clear the molten liquid away. If you move the hot wire around, the hole can be made bigger. With practice you can develop a good degree of control over the shape of the hole.

You may wish to model flat, concave or convex forms which are little thicker than sheet, but nevertheless modelled sufficiently to require the use of inlay or carving wax. If so you can spread your wax onto a thin piece of dry investment plaster (see figs 140 and 141), or a piece of investment plaster that has been immersed for a short time in molten wax. The wax model and the plaster base will later be embedded in a casting flask. All manner of hollow objects may be made using this technique. You can save a lot of time by applying the wax to a pre-formed, rigid base, instead of trying to build up a form with a modelling tool. You can also model a tubular form, or a deep vessel with an opening at one end, or even a spherical shape, providing that it has a few holes in the surface. First of all you must make a core from dry investment plaster. Its outer dimensions must be identical to the inner dimensions of your design. Spread the wax over the core and complete the surface modelling. If you were now to embed the model and the core in investment plaster and melt out the wax you can imagine that the core might move to one side of the cavity and ruin the casting. You can prevent this from happening at the stage when you have finished modelling the wax. Put a 1·5 mm (0·0591 in.) drill into a pin vice and carefully drill a hole right through the wax model and the core. Now pass a 1·5 mm (0·0591 in.) wire of the metal which you intend to use for the casting through the hole and allow it to project 10 mm (0·394 in.) on either side of the model. Some distance away, drill another hole at right angles to the first and insert another wire with the same projections. When the model and the wires are embedded in a flask, the core will be held in position whilst casting proceeds. You may also use a plaster core when you model a ring, making the core the same diameter as the finger that is to wear it. Some people find this a much easier way of modelling, but others prefer to model rings on a metal triblet, warming the triblet when the model is to be removed. I use a plaster former because the whole thing is easily handled and is light in weight. When you shape plaster cores use an old file or emery cloth because plaster will blunt and ruin a new file. It is not usually necessary to mix investment plaster specially to make cores because you will almost always have some left in your mixing bowl after investing a flask, and this can be left to set and then kept until needed.

You can also use found materials in investment castings and providing a material will melt or burn out of plaster anything can be cast. Included in this category is wood bark and any natural form, although leaves, for instance, would need backing with wax to make them thick enough. You might also want to use parts of plastic figures, or even a glued collage of sections of plastic building bricks.

It is now necessary to consider the setting up of the model so that it can be embedded in investment plaster for casting. To do this you must attach to the model a series of wax wires called sprues, which are brought together and fastened to a sprue base on which will be placed a casting flask. Mix investment plaster and pour it into the flask, level with the top.

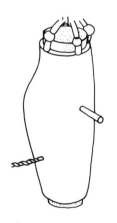

Fig. 143 Wax model shaped on a core. One core wire is already in place, and the hole for the other is being drilled

79

When it is set break off the sprue base to reveal the sprue or sprues through which the molten wax will empty and metal will enter. Different casting techniques demand different sprue sizes. Steam pressure, vacuum, and hand-swung centrifugal casting methods have sprues which must be no larger in diameter than 1·5 mm (0·0591 in.), while machine centrifugal casting can use much larger sprues. In the case of steam pressure, vacuum, and hand-swung centrifugal casting the metal is melted in a depression in the top of the casting flask. The sprue base or plate may be conical; if it is attach the sprues directly to the cone, spacing them 2 or 3 mm (about 0·1 in.) apart. If you have no conical base you can use a flat one and bring the sprues together to form one large sprue. When the flask has been invested and broken off the plate, the investment plaster must be carved back into a conical depression until the separate sprue ends are revealed.

Fig. 144 Wax model and sprue attached to a rubber sprue base

Before setting up your model on sprues and investing it you must select a suitable casting flask. Ideally it will be made from stainless steel, but it can be mild steel, preferably with a wall thickness of 1·5 mm (0·0591 in.). The flask must be large enough for the model to have a 10 mm (0·394 in.) clearance between it and the walls. The model must also be set at least 10 mm (0·394 in.) below the surface of the plaster at one end and about 40 mm (1·575 in.) should be allowed for the sprues and the depression in which the metal is melted at the other end. Before you start to cut and attach sprues draw a simple full-size side elevation of the model in its can so that you can work out all the clearances. There is nothing more irritating than setting a model up on its sprues and base, only to find that it projects way above the top of the can. You should attach your sprues to the heaviest parts of the model, always to the back of the model if possible, and certainly to points which are easily cleaned up. You can use commercial sprues or if this seems too expensive roll your own. Use a soft beeswax substitute and slice off a sliver that you can squeeze into a rough sausage shape you can then roll to size on the bench with your fingers. Alternatively, you can make a good sprue maker by converting an old grease gun. Modify the nozzle to the correct hole size, fill the gun with soft wax, and then warm it until a wax wire can be extruded.

Fig. 145 Can with sprue base removed to show sprue ends

To attach a sprue to your model, warm a modelling tool, place the sprue at the correct angle in position on the model and insert the tip of the modelling tool between the sprue and the model. The waxes will melt and weld together. Check the join carefully and seal it with molten wax if necessary. It is a good idea to build up a blob of wax on each sprue at a point approximately 4 mm (0·158 in.) from the model. The blobs act as reservoirs of molten metal during casting, so that if the sprues cool before the model, metal will not be drawn from the model leaving ruinous porosity around the base. At this stage you must weigh the model and multiply its weight by the specific gravity of the metal to be used, e.g., silver by 10·5. The answer indicates the weight of metal necessary for the casting.

Fig. 146 Wax model and sprues attached to a flat metal base

Now attach the model and the sprues to the sprue base. Sprue bases made of rubber can be purchased in varying sizes and you need only push the casting flask into the sealing sleeve before filling it with investment plaster. If, however, you use a metal plate or base, the casting flask must

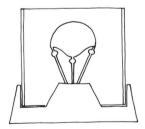

Fig. 147 It is important to work out clearances between bottom and sides of the casting can and the model

Fig. 148 Attach sprues to the wax model with a hot modelling tool

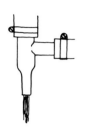

Fig. 149 Casting rig outlet

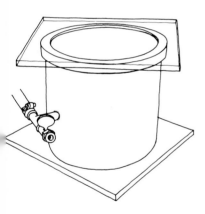

Fig. 150 Put acrylic sheet over your vacuum tank

be sealed to it with soft wax and a hot modelling tool.

Fill the casting flask with investment plaster; ordinary plaster of Paris will not under any circumstances be suitable. Plaster manufacturers will supply you with data regarding the correct proportions of plaster and water, but most people mix by 'feel' and experience. I use a rule of thumb method which allows for a little plaster to be left after the flask has been filled. Assuming the casting flask is sealed to the sprue base and the model is in place, fill the flask to seven eighths of its capacity with cold water. Pour the water into a flexible plastic or rubber bowl and add investment plaster, mixing constantly with one hand until you have a thick creamy consistency. Carefully pour the plaster into the casting flask and leave it to set for one to four hours, according to the size of the casting flask, before applying any heat. It is a good idea to lessen the surface tension of the model by painting it with a soap solution so that air bubbles do not easily adhere to it. The tendency for air bubbles to spoil a casting can be eliminated by building up a layer of investment plaster on the model with a paint brush and allowing it to set before finally filling the casting flask. Air in the investment plaster can also be lessened by rocking and tapping the flask, or placing it on a vibrator, but the most effective method is to use a vacuum tank. You can buy a simple vacuum tank which uses the domestic water supply or you can construct one using brazing or welding equipment. The rig consists of a tubular tank 170 mm (6·693 in.) in diameter and 170 mm high with a double outlet on one side. One outlet has a tap and the other has a tube, leading to a venturi valve which is also attached to the cold water tap. Water passes through the valve drawing air from the vacuum tank. Place a piece of transparent acrylic sheet over the top of the vacuum tank so that you can watch the casting flask as air is extracted. A rubber gasket must be fitted to the top of the tank, or to the acrylic sheet to ensure a perfect seal between them and an efficient vacuum. Before investing the flask you must attach a paper collar around the top and seal it with tape; then pour in the investment, which should have a little proprietary de-bubblizer added, and place the can in the vacuum tank. Put the acrylic top in place, turn on the water tap and rock the tank gently but continuously. Bubbles will rise to the surface of the investment, and gradually the whole investment will rise up inside the paper collar and will appear to boil. After a while the plaster will sink back, the tap on the side of the tank can be opened, the acrylic sheet removed, and the flask taken out and left to set. The whole operation from mixing the plaster, to finishing the vacuum process should not take more than nine minutes.

The wax must now be burnt out of the investment plaster, and for small casting flasks this can be done quite adequately in a small and comparatively inexpensive enamelling kiln. For the sophisticated workshop it is of course possible to buy a custom built burn-out kiln. The flask should first of all be placed, sprue ends downwards, in front of the kiln, so that the wax can gradually run out and the moisture is slowly driven off. When this is achieved turn the flask so that the sprue ends are uppermost and place it in the kiln. Remove the flask at intervals and look down the sprue holes. When they glow red it is time to begin casting. Do not on any account allow the whole flask to become bright red, because the plaster

Fig. 151 Attach a paper collar to your casting can before you fill it with investment plaster

will crack and deteriorate.

To cast your model using vacuum pressure you will need some way of tapping the vacuum in the equipment that has already been described. The simplest rig consists of two round plates with holes in the centre connected by a pipe with a tap in the middle. Place the device on top of the vacuum chamber, close the tap between the plates, and build up a vacuum in the tank. Place a soft asbestos mat with a hole in the centre in the middle of the top plate and put the hot casting flask on it. Cut the correct weight of metal into small pieces and place it in the depression in the top of the flask, melt it with a gas torch. Add a pinch of borax as the metal melts and sustain the heat until it becomes a molten pool. Continuing to apply heat, open the tap between the plates and the vacuum will suck the metal down the sprue holes into the main mould. The metal will not flow down the sprue holes by gravity because they are so narrow; the surface tension of the metal is your ally here, and this is why it is essential that the sprues should not be more than 1·5 mm (0·0591 in.) in diameter. If, before casting, you notice a crack in the bottom of the investment plaster, burnish it with a smooth piece of metal, such as a modelling tool. The casting may have a flash on it afterwards, but at least the metal should not be drawn through the bottom of the investment. After casting leave the flask to cool until the metal button that is visible in the top of the plaster has lost its red colour, and then plunge the whole thing into a bucket of water. Most of the investment plaster will erupt and fall away. If you quench the casting too soon the thermal shock may crack the metal.

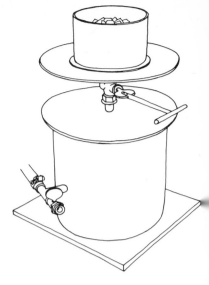

Fig. 152 Vacuum casting rig with can in place

The hand-swung centrifugal process is a more spectacular method of casting, and utilizes equipment that is very easy to make if a centrifugal casting machine is not available. You need a cradle with a hole in the bottom and a bucket type of handle at the top. This hooks onto a length of chain which terminates in a pivot at the end of a handle. The cradle must be strong, constructed from 2 mm (0·079 in.) steel with an equally strong handle. The hook and chain must also be well constructed. When the flask is hot, place it in the cradle, hang the cradle on the chain, and add the correct quantity of metal. Stand with the arm that holds the handle of the casting rig extended downwards and heat the metal in the top of the flask with a gas torch. When it is molten swing the flask smoothly in a vertical arc, over and over for a dozen or so revolutions. The centrifugal force to which the metal is subject will force it down the sprue holes and into the mould. This method is suitable for small quantities of metal such as are needed for rings. It is vital to make the depression in the top of the casting flask deep enough to hold the metal easily, otherwise you will spill metal all round the workshop.

Steam pressure casting involves a rig that can be built in a workshop with engineering equipment, or to your specification at a small engineering workshop. The rig consists of a steel base plate with a vertical pillar at one side. Pivoted from the top of the pillar is a metal bar with a handle at the end. Part way along the bar, and in a position where it will swing down over the centre of the base plate, there hangs and pivots a shallow, circular, inverted container. Pack the container with wet asbestos paper pulp. Position the hot casting flask on an asbestos pad on the base plate,

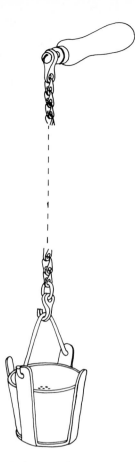

so that the handle of the rig can be lowered until the inverted container can be clamped over it. Put your metal into the casting flask and melt it. Continuing to apply heat, clamp the container over the flask. The heat of the metal will generate steam from the wet asbestos, pressure will build up and the metal will be forced into the mould. Each different size of casting flask must be positioned, and the base plate marked with chalk, before you start the burning out of the flask, because if the asbestos container is not clamped swiftly and accurately the pressure is not generated completely and the casting fails.

Silver and gold can be cast by all the methods that have been described, but bronze is unsuitable for steam pressure casting because hydrogen is produced, and a craterous cast results.

When the casting has been broken out of the investment plaster, and scrubbed with a stiff brush, it can be heated and quenched in cold water to remove any remaining plaster. It should then be placed in a strong solution of a proprietary non-acid pickle, or in a dilute solution of hydrofluoric acid to clean the metal. Clip or saw off the sprues as close to the model as possible and proceed with whatever finishing techniques you need to meet your design.

Fig. 153   Hand-swung
centrifugal casting rig
showing can in place

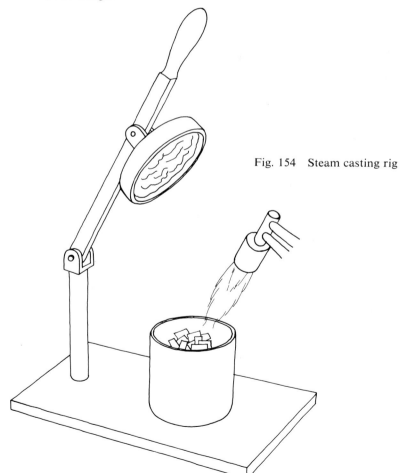

Fig. 154   Steam casting rig

Cuttlefish casting is a technique which can be exploited to good effect. Cuttlefish bone can be obtained at some jewellers' and silversmiths' suppliers, and at pet shops. The bone must be in quite large pieces, and if you can buy a whole piece you can cut it in half with a hacksaw. Before you can do this you must flatten the soft, powdery side by rubbing it down on emery or sandpaper on a flat plate. Now place the bone flat face down, and slowly saw through the hard outer shell of the back. Do not hurry this stage or you will shatter the bone. Carve a negative impression or mould of your design in the flat soft face of the cuttlefish bone. You must carve at least 30 mm (1·181 in.) from the sawn end of the bone because a funnel-shaped entry, wide enough for the metal to be poured in easily, must be cut and there must be a good weight of metal pressing into the mould to give a sharp definition to the casting. When you have cut the mould, brush its surface with a paint brush; a distinctive texture will appear. Cuttlefish bone consists of alternate layers of hard membrane and soft powdery material. When you brush the surface of your mould the powder is cleared away between the membranes, leaving ridges which flow and vary according to the angle at which you have cut into the bone. You can exploit this quality in an attractive way as your experience of the technique grows. The dispersal of air as metal flows into the mould is achieved by cutting fine radial grooves from the edge of the mould towards the outer edge of the cuttlefish bone. The grooves should fade out before reaching the edge of the bone or molten metal may leak from the mould. It is often helpful, with an intricate mould, to cut riser channels from prominent parts of the design, going up to the top of the cuttlefish bone alongside the entry funnel. If you have cut the tolerances a bit fine, you can pack wet asbestos or wet tissue paper around the suspect joints.

Wire the cuttlefish up to a flat block of compressed charcoal, enclosing the mould and making it ready to receive the hot metal. Melt the metal in a charcoal block that has been hollowed at one end, and has a pouring channel. Hold the block in tongs during the melting process, and gently tip it over the cuttlefish mould. Metal may also be melted in a graphite crucible, a crucible furnace or a blacksmith's forge. The metal must be poured in a smooth, quick action, or it will cool too much to give a sharp casting, and may not even find its way around an intricate mould.

Existing objects can be pressed into cuttlefish bone if you want to reproduce them, and if you want to make a double sided casting press the object to be reproduced into one piece of cuttlefish to half its depth. On either side and below the pressed mould sink three ball-bearings into the bone, once again to half their depth. Now press another piece of cuttlefish bone onto the projecting forms until it closes up to the first piece of bone; lift it off. Take out the object to be reproduced, cut a pouring funnel, and put the mould together again. The ball-bearings will ensure that the two halves register together. Wire them up and proceed as above.

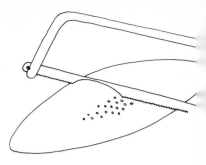

Fig. 155 Cuttlefish can be cut to size

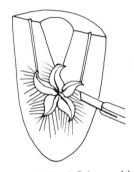

Fig. 156 Cuttlefish moulds should be cut with risers and air vents

Fig. 157 Melt silver in a piece of charcoal before you pour it into a cuttlefish mould

84

13 Finishing

Finishing – the trueing and refining of forms – is a vital stage in the production of holloware and jewelry. This process will decide whether you produce an ordinary object or a superb one. Finishing requires great concentration and a mind alert to the fact that every action you take affects the finished article. For instance, if you have a small cut or scratch on the surface of a piece of metal, and you file and polish only that point, you will create a hollow which catches the light and ruins the appearance of your design. As most jobs have several pits and scratches you will end up with a very patchy object if you are not careful. Instead, you should remove the blemish, and carefully grade away the hollow, cleaning down quite a wide area of metal so that no hollow is left. Should a blemish be filed away, or should it be filled? Can you afford to remove precious metal, and, in doing so, will you weaken the structure of your job?

The tools and equipment generally used in finishing are files of different sorts, abrasive cloths and papers, and abrasive stones, such as water of Ayr stone. You need files in a variety of sizes and a silversmith or jeweller should keep a basic collection of 15-cm (6-in.) and 10-cm (4-in.) files in both fine and medium grades. A silversmith might also keep a few coarse 15-cm (6-in.) files. Flat or hand files are universally useful, and usually have cutting surfaces on both wide faces and on one edge. The edge without cutting teeth is most useful because you can file right into a corner, and remove metal from one side of it only. Half-round files are always tapered, and the pointed rather than stub-ended ones are essential. In addition, square, triangular and round files are needed from time to time. A square or triangular file is, for instance, often a better tool for trueing a shallow concave form than a half-round file.

In addition, every silversmith and jeweller must keep a complete set of needle files, though some shapes will be used far more often than others, and will need replacing individually. The most useful are those with an oval section, and a rat-tail section with teeth on the flat face only. Needle files must be stocked in at least two grades, say grades 1 and 2, and the jeweller may well require something much finer. A selection of escapement files may also be needed by the jeweller for the finest and most delicate work. It is also useful to have one or two rifflers (files with curved ends), because there are often awkward spots that cannot be reached with any straight file. The most useful riffler has a triangular section at one end and an oval section at the other. Rifflers can be obtained in a variety of grades and are comparatively expensive.

Filing is the first stage in finishing. Begin only after careful consideration

Fig. 158   Riffler file

of the task to be performed, which will depend on the skill and care that you have exercised with previous processes. It would be absurd, for example, for you to undertake a major filing job with a fine needle file; on the other hand if you attack a small local blemish with a coarse, 15-cm (6-in.) file, you may make much worse blemishes over a large area, and suffer a time-consuming set back. This often happens to the beginner, and it is at this stage that common sense comes into its own. You can establish the size of file for a job by selecting one that seems too fine to start with. File the surface for a while and then inspect it. If the effect has been negligible you must choose the next coarser grade of file. The beginner often tries to polish a surface on which coarse file marks have not been completely removed with an intermediate abrasive or fine file. This need not happen if you change the direction of your filing when you use the fine file, and cross over the coarse file marks at right angles. Using this method the coarse marks show up plainly until they are removed. You can also hold your work up to the light and tilt it backwards and forwards so that any trace of the deep marks are highlighted.

The way in which you use your file is most important. The most economical and efficient cut is obtained by filing diagonally from left to right, pushing away and sideways to make a cut, and pulling the file back lightly before pushing off for another cut. This action covers the maximum ground for energy expended, and leaves the cleanest, smoothest possible cut. If you push your file straight backwards and forwards, you will tend to cut a channel in your metal, and produce a scored, rough surface. If you want a flat surface you must not rock the file, or you will curve the surface and round the edges of the work. You must lock your wrists and file with great care and precision, checking the surface frequently with a square. If you are filing on a curved surface you must follow the form with a flowing, diagonal wrist action, so that facets and grooves are eliminated.

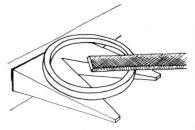

Fig. 159 Ring filed flat on a bench pin

Holding work is often difficult because boxes and curved holloware or tapered and curved solid sections can be badly marked or distorted if you hold them in a vice. If it is possible to use a vice, use padded or soft jaws and if the position of the work has to be changed, clean all surfaces to remove loose filings before tightening up the vice again. Filings which are pressed into polished surfaces cause deep pits and a demoralizing amount of repair work. You will, in fact, find that it is best to hold most forms by hand when you are filing them, because you can see the whole form and you can sit and work with the metal at a bench pin at a comfortable eye level. The bench pin is most important as an aid to holding work. Its V form is an excellent point for wedging work, and when it is turned over so that its sloping surface is below the bench top, you can rest your work on it and use the edge of the bench as a pressure point. You may file nicks and grooves in the pin as an aid to holding all sorts of forms steady while you file them. The most ineffective methods of filing and finishing involve holding the work in one hand, or resting it on one knee, whilst using the file in the other hand. These are methods often used by the less dedicated, who want to move across to their neighbours' bench for a chat.

Always work systematically across a surface that needs filing; do not

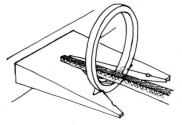

Fig. 160 Ring held in grooves cut into the bench pin so that you can file the inside surface

86

jump from place to place because you will never produce a true form in that way. Filing into a corner to produce a true and neat angle is not easy. I have already mentioned that you can use a flat file with a smooth edge, but this is of little help if you do not have the technique to use it. You should push the file along the corner line, and then diagonally away from it so that the corner is sharpened, and the metal which runs away from it is kept flat and true. A similar job on a piece of jewelry should be done with a knife edge needle file. Finishing sometimes begins before a job is soldered together, and during the course of construction you must decide when the soldering together of components is going to make subsequent finishing and polishing difficult to carry out. For instance, if a long spout is to be soldered to a coffee pot, then you might well make sure that the facing surfaces of the spout and the body are free from blemishes and are polished before soldering is carried out. Similarly, the inside of a metal handle and the side of the body to which it is to be soldered must be polished. If you are soldering intricate jewelry parts or pierced sheet over hollowed forms, pre-finishing and polishing must be carried out. You need to think ahead all the time, and you must think about your finishing problems at the time of designing. If you must have polished surfaces behind pierced forms, perhaps you had better use miniature bolts or some similar device to hold the components together. In all pre-polishing operations, the polish will appear to be lost during subsequent solderings, but the real hard work, which is difficult to do in a confined space, will have been done and the polish can be restored fairly easily.

A problem which often confronts the craftsman during the finishing stages is the discovery of pinholes or slightly dry solder joints. It is worth remembering that these problems usually arise as a result of attempting to solder badly fitted joints in the first place. Obviously such blemishes must be removed, however near you are to finishing a piece of work. The apparently obvious and easy solution is to simply fill all pits and faults with more solder. This may be successful if the pin hole was caused by a little dirt that pickle will remove, but if the hole was too large to hold solder in the first place, it will only run away during a second application and probably reappear somewhere else as an awkward blob or pool that is difficult to remove. It is much better to enlarge the hole with a drill and then plug it with a close fitting wire before adding solder. Similarly, a dry joint in a wire that has been soldered into or around a body can be slotted with a saw and a piece of sheet soldered into place. Repairing pinholes in silver involves one special worry for the craftsman. When silver has been subject to several applications of heat, as in soldering and annealing, it develops a layer of fire stain on the surface. This is a grey colour and is caused by the copper in the alloy oxidizing on the surface. During the normal finishing and polishing process the fire stain is removed, but if you discover a pinhole or dry joint at this time you are faced with the prospect of staining the silver all over again. As this means cleaning the whole job down again you might decide to live with the pinhole. The problem can be overcome by mixing thick borax and coating the whole piece of work with it. Heat it slowly and paint more borax on those areas from which it is drawing away; when it is completely covered proceed with the soldering. Air will be kept from the surface of the metal and no oxidization and fire staining can take place. There are proprietary brands of firestain preventive on the market which should be used as directed by the manufacturers.

When you have finished filing proceed to finer abrasives such as emery cloths and papers, or silica carbide papers for dry or wet use. An equally important abrasive is water of Ayr stone. The general aim at this stage is to continue the work of trueing surfaces, and to make sure that ripples and streaks do not appear because they will ruin a fine, polished surface.

The polishing papers and cloths will generally give best value if they are glued to sticks or boards. If you hold paper in your hand it will quickly crease and tear and last no time at all. Every craftsman should have a range of sticks of different widths with various grades of paper upon them. The edges of the sticks can be chamfered to give access to corners and narrow places on designs. The cutting quality of emery polishing paper is indicated by numbers on the back of the paper. Grades 1, 1-0, 2-0, and crocus paper are useful qualities to keep. Some craftsmen prefer 'wet and dry' papers and once again the grit size can be found on the back of the paper. Grit sizes 320, 400, and 600 are the most suitable. It is worth saying that some craftsmen think that grit tends to become embedded in the metal when this paper is used, and causes drag marks during subsequent polishing. Certainly 'wet and dry' paper should be used with plenty of water, which must be changed very regularly. In working surfaces with emery sticks observe all the rules laid down for filing if you wish to develop true and polished surfaces.

A good method of cleaning some surfaces is to use a strip of emery polishing paper placed in a slotted spindle which is held in the chuck of a flexible-drive polishing motor. As the spindle revolves the paper coils around it, but the end flails and flies wide. As the spindle is brought to the work surface the paper begins to polish, and pressure will speed up the rate of abrasion and polishing. It is a most effective technique for the insides of rings, and can be used on flat surfaces with care. The beginner will tend to ripple the surface slightly, and should finally finish work with a stick.

Fig. 161   Cleaning ring on the inside surface with polishing paper and a pendant polishing motor

Water of Ayr stone can be used for all the tasks that paper is used for, except in the case of very fine papers which produce quite a high polish. Many, perhaps most, craftsmen prefer a water of Ayr stone to finish a box, and for cleaning down corners between bezels and box edges. The most important attribute of stone is that it has a firm, hard surface and can be placed most precisely to deal with awkward problems. The surface of a stone makes it ideal for trueing the sides and top of a box, because it does not round the edges and corners. Not only does this destroy the look of a box, but it may wear away the solder joints and pin holes may appear. A stone should be used with plenty of clean water, and the work area must be swept to remove all grit. The work should be rested on a cloth so that the under surface is not scratched. When stoning a box select a long, wide stone and work with long, diagonal movements across the surface.

If hollows appear, usually emphasized by patches of fine stain in silver, you must test them against a straight edge to see how deep they are. Place

Fig. 162　Burnisher

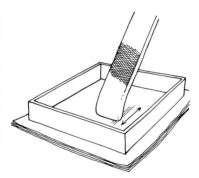

Fig. 163　Rest a box on
several layers of paper to
burnish it

the straight edge over the hollow; if you see light under the edge the hollow is too deep to remove by stoning because you will have to remove metal from the rest of the surface on which it is situated. This will be costly in time and metal and the structure of the job may be weakened. It is best to burnish the offending spot from the inside of the box and so raise the surface. The burnisher should be made from a large, old, flat file. Bend the end into a gentle curve, round the sharp edges and polish the whole end. Put the box, offending side downwards, on several sheets of paper on a flat plate. Pour some soap solution onto the back of the hollow, ask someone to hold the box steady, and rub the burnisher backwards and forwards over the back of the hollow. You may have to apply some pressure, but the metal will be stretched and pushed, the paper will give where you apply the pressure and the box will lose its hollow. You can then continue stoning until all fire stain has been removed.

A box is always stoned with its lid in place, and you must aim to produce a surface so true that only a fine line indicates where the opening takes place. For stoning awkward places such as corners, between settings in jewelry, or narrow gaps, you may need a very thin or chamfered stone. You can cut or alter a stone with an old saw blade or an old file. Never use new equipment because you will spoil it in the process.

Finally you must realize that finishing is a comparatively slow job and that finishing and polishing can between them account for one third of the total production time of any piece of work.

14 Polishing

Polishing is the continuation of the process which begins when files, polishing papers and water of Ayr stones are used to develop a progressively finer surface on your metal. It is a technique which can make or mar your work. Careless polishing or the use of polishing techniques in an attempt to remove serious blemishes, bumps and deep file marks can only result in the removal of all crisp edges and the substitution of a slurred and sloppy form, streaked with drag marks and directional grooves.

Polishing can be split into two main systems; hand methods and machine methods. Generally speaking, machine methods are quite essential to the silversmith, but there are many who feel that most of the work on jewelry should be done by hand, using a soft mop, perhaps, to give a final sheen on certain types of work. Hand polishing involves the use of wooden sticks to which you should glue various grades of leather so that a progressively high polish can be reached. The polishing mediums for use with the sticks include rouge and tripoli compounds which can be rubbed onto the surface of the leather. Use polishing sticks in the same way as a file or an emery stick, working in all directions with a flowing, wrist action for curved surfaces and a firm, locked wrist action for flat surfaces. Many craftsmen use a lubricant with a leather stick to prevent the surface clogging with compound and becoming scaly with metal that has been removed from the surface of the work, and may leave scratches on the polished metal. Use liquid metal polish or paraffin for this. If you have no lubricant you must scrape the leather at regular intervals with a sharp piece of metal sheet. Where there is no access for a polishing stick you can use strips of cloth or soft string. One end of the cloth or string should be held in a vice or pinned to the bench (fig. 164) and the other end held in one hand. Pull the material taut, rub the appropriate compound on it – tripoli for hard work, or rouge for finishing – and swiftly rub your job backwards and forwards along its length. Do not polish continuously in one place, because you will cut a groove into the metal. Instead, move your work about as much as possible, twisting and turning it so that you develop an even polish. This system can be used in narrow clefts in holloware, as in the joint between a body and spout, or a body and handle, or for polishing the edges of pierced holes in sheet metal. It is also a most useful method for polishing jewelry, including pierced work, claw settings, or wirework.

Another method of hand polishing involves the use of a hardened steel or agate burnisher. Old files, which can be softened, bent to any necessary shape, rounded at the edges and the end, and then polished and hardened,

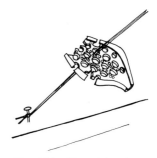

Fig. 164   Use string to polish small holes

make excellent burnishers. The burnisher must be lubricated with saliva, soap solution, or liquid detergent, and then rubbed backwards and forwards on the metal progressively covering the surface. A high polish can easily be built up on strip and wire work, but you do need skill to burnish a large, flat surface without making ridges.

Machine polishing involves the use of polishing motors, described in Chapter 1. The work is done with wheels of leather or hard felt of various thicknesses and diameters, or with mops of coarse or soft cloth. Different sets of mops should be kept for different metals and for plastics, and it is a good idea to have a colour code on the centre of the mops to denote their different purposes. Most mops consist of many circles of cloth clamped together between fibre washers and secured by nails. When a mop revolves on the polishing motor, centrifugal force stiffens the layers of cloth, so that the mop seems a solid but resilient wheel. Coarse mops are made from unbleached calico and are impregnated with a dressing which gives then a fast cutting quality. Medium grade mops are made from untreated calico, and soft mops are made from cotton, and can be positively identified by the soft swansdown pile on one side of each individual circle of cloth. In addition to these mops there are others made from many radial strands of cotton or wool for imparting the finest finish of all.

Brushes are also available to aid the finishing and polishing processes. They have wood or plastic centres with the bristles arranged in various ways. Some have bristles arranged radially like the spokes of a wheel; some have bristles which project from the end of the centre boss for cleaning into flat bottoms inside holloware; and some have bristles arranged around a domed centre boss, like hairs on a head, and are used for cleaning the sides and rounded bottoms of holloware. Brass wire brushes are also available in similar shapes and sizes.

As interiors should always be finished before exteriors, I will describe interior polishing first. Bottom brushes and round-headed brushes can be used to produce a soft and uniform satin finish inside work. The cleaning medium is sometimes a rather evil mixture of oil and pumice powder which is mixed to a thick consistency. Ladle some of the mixture into your piece of work, start the polishing motor, place your work over the brush and slowly revolve it against the direction of the motor. The work and the mixture will become hot, the mixture will become thin, the pumice will scour the interior of the work, and you will become oily and dirty.

For a cleaner and more attractive technique, and for exterior use, the revolving brush can be run against a bar of brushing emery compound, and then applied to the metal. Large workshops can use the Lea compound system in which a glue bond is applied to the bristles and then a bar of the grit of your choice. Leave the brush running so that the compound sets, then play it over the surface of the metal. If you use the brush too soon, the compound can stick to the metal, and prove difficult to remove.

If you wish to work up a slightly finer satin finish on interiors or exteriors you can use a brass scratch brush. You must use soapy water as a lubricant, and only the lightest of pressures on your work, or an ugly, dull, brass deposit will be bonded onto your work. There are also commercial (Scotchbrite) wheels which do no work in removing blemishes, but provide a fine satin finish. When you want an immaculate satin finish you should achieve a perfect polish first, and then break the surface down to the degree of satin finish that you require. A satin finish that is too coarse is prone to ugly water and grease staining. The perfect satin finish is probably one in which you can see your face faintly if you get very, very close to the surface – the application of such a finish is a very skilled business.

The simplest routine with mops involves the use of three grades of mop. First of all, quick cutting can be achieved with a 15 cm (5·905 in.) diameter coarse calico mop which is reinforced with dressing. The mop should be placed on the polishing motor and run against a coarse wire brush (fig. 165) or the sharpened end of a flat file to remove all dried polish and metal scale, and also to ensure that the mop is quite circular. The polishing medium for quick cutting and polishing is tripoli compound, in bar form, and it should be applied to the revolving mop for a moment to prime it (fig. 166). You then apply your work to the surface of the mop, just below the level of the spindle (fig. 167) so that the surface is moving away from you. If you have the work snatched from your hand by the drag of the mop, it will fall downwards and away from you. Never attempt to save your work, let it go rather than risk serious injury. Never hook your hand through handles or loops. Keep long hair tied up, take off scarves or ties or tuck them away in overalls, and do not wear loose, baggy clothes that can be caught in the mop.

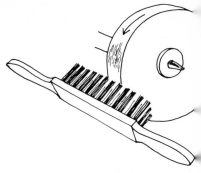

Fig. 165   Use a wire brush to clean your polishing mop

If you are polishing a box, plate, or lid, work from the centre downwards towards the lower edge. Then turn the work and polish another section, still working from the centre downwards, until you have polished the whole surface. Always polish down to the edges; never work from the centre up to an edge because as the mop is moving downwards it will snatch at the edge and pull the work from your hands. It is terrifying to see a beginner polishing above the level of the spindle, or even almost on top of the mop. If you do this, your work can be hurled at you by a mop which may have a surface speed of 1,400 metres per minute. Finally don't talk to anyone as you work and, if anyone talks to you, switch off the motor or tell them to go away, because polishing on a powerful motor requires great concentration.

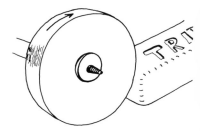

Fig. 166   Apply polishing compound to a polishing mop

When you are polishing with a mop you must apply a noticeable pressure if you are to achieve an improvement in the finish. If progress seems slow, press harder. If you are working on a narrow surface or into a corner, or simply finding that the mop drags, you may find it easier to apply one edge of the mop and ease the full face onto the metal as your confidence grows. Handles, spouts, and other projections are always a problem and you must exercise caution and keep the projections pointing downwards. After you have completely polished your work with the coarse mop, inspect it for pits, drag marks and file marks. All such blemishes must be scraped or stoned, or both, because it is simply no use polishing away at a fault and hoping to remove it. Even if you can do so, you will certainly spoil some part of your work, and it will take you much longer than scraping or stoning. Once the polish is perfect at this stage, you can use the softer calico mop with tripoli and then move onto a cotton swansdown

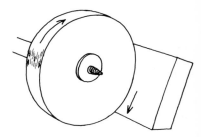

Fig. 167   Polishing a flat metal surface

mop using rouge compound. Soft mops drag and grab at your work far more readily than hard ones, and many a job has been lost in the final stages – so beware!

Hard felt wheels can be used for cleaning fire stain off your work, instead of a stone. The cutting medium is a sand, such as Trent sand, which you must scoop up with one hand from a box on the bench beneath the polishing wheel. Hold the work in your other hand and feed the sand on top of the bob; it will be drawn past the metal, cutting the surface away very quickly. This is a skilled and dirty job, and the beginner should practice on scrap pieces. Felt bobs used with tripoli are very useful for reaching into the corners of box bezels, and other angular positions, and you can cut all sorts of angles and curves on the cutting surface of the bob, using an old file that has been sharpened like a turning tool. A bullet-shaped bob can be used to polish inside spoon bowls, small wine cups, hollowed sheet jewelry, and other rounded forms. Some craftsmen use a wide and carefully trimmed felt bob for the early polishing stages on a box, because it does not wrap around, and round off, the edges. However, others claim that it produces faint ripples on the metal surface and prefer stoning, hand polishing, and careful work with a mop.

Jewelry polishing often utilizes bench polishing motors, which need to be smaller than those found in a silversmithing shop. Miniature versions of the polishing mops, bobs, and brushes described above are available for use with pendant polishing motors (see Chapter 1) with flexible drive shafts and collet chucks.

Barrel polishing is worth considering for small items and modest jewelry, even in a small workshop, and certainly in a school where polishing is a serious problem with young children. Basically, barrel polishing is carried out in a plastic container or a glass jar which must be filled to between half and three quarters of its capacity with round metal balls, ovals, needles or other shapes, together with water and a soap powder. The work is placed in the container with the soap and polishing shapes, and revolved at 60 revolutions per minute for two or three hours. The metal shapes slide across the work, and the work slides across the shapes constantly as the barrel revolves so that the work is gradually burnished. Custom built jewelry barrel polishers can be bought, though they are not cheap, but inexpensive stone-tumbling polishers in which the drum revolves on rollers are used by some home workers. If the drum seems too light to revolve properly with only jewelry and ball-bearings in it, put two large rubber bands around the barrel so that the rollers can grip the surface. The result of barrel polishing, in connoisseurs' terms, is a rather bright but brittle polish that needs further hand or mop polishing if a subtle finish is to be attained. Flat surfaces are polished with round balls, but tend to show a speckled surface of many, many, shallow dents, while wire work should be polished with needle shapes. Perhaps the ideal work for barrel polishing, as far as the serious jeweller is concerned, is textured cast work, or wire work.

15 Design

Design is an emotive word and an emotive subject. A particular piece of silver or jewelry will, if viewed by a variety of people, evoke expressions of admiration or contempt according to personal standpoints. It seems, therefore, that the act of designing embraces, at the highest level, personal philosophies and principles that the practitioners hold very dearly. Knowledge of this sensitive and emotional background to designing makes life very difficult for the beginner, especially when he or she can see that it is also of great advantage to possess some facility in the craft of drawing so that ideas can be recorded and pushed around with reasonable ease.

This chapter aims to help the beginner find confidence in approaching design for silversmithing and jewelry. It may help to separate the ingredients of design in the hope that you may recognize an area in which you have a personal strength or talent, and through which you can build an all-round ability as a designer.

For instance, if you are a very practical person with a good knowledge of metals and what they will do for you, it is absurd to throw all that knowledge overboard, and to indulge in an irrational search for an original, 'artistic' solution, which will probably result in an inappropriate use of material, and an impractical object of bizarre appearance. It would be much better to produce an honest, practical object to which you can apply simple principles of proportion and scale, and to which you can gradually add new qualities as your experience grows.

Appearance, beauty, aesthetics, and fashion are some of the words that describe what concerns many people when they talk about design and these are indeed most important. This part of designing is best interpreted by drawing. If you are to produce an object in three dimensions, possibly in an expensive material, and of exactly the form that you require, the quickest way to develop the picture in your mind is as a picture on paper. All this presupposes that you are clever or lucky enough, or sufficiently imaginative to have a clear picture in your mind. It is more likely that you will have only a rough idea of what you want and that you will have to draw it, look at it and compare it mentally to the idea that you thought you had, and then think again and re-draw it until you have produced what you wanted, or you realize that it is no basis for an idea after all and that it should be forgotten. The forms or images upon which you base your jewelry or silver are not simply plucked, as if by magic, from a special and talented brain; they are the result of experience, of observation, of mental assessment of everything around you. They may be based upon natural forms, for example. The use of natural form can be arbitarily divided into representational or photographic images on the one hand, and the abstracted or selected forms therein, on the other. There is no particular case for arguing for or against realism or abstraction, though fashion and current trends may weigh heavily here. In the case of jewelry, fashion is now less of a taskmaster, and people often wear what they like best or what they feel suits them. You may find, however, that realism, though presenting severe technical challenges, will pall eventually and that you will be drawn into the challenge of abstraction to a lesser or greater degree. You will discover that it is only when you begin to isolate the essence or heart of an image, that many people will credit you with the effort of designing.

Natural form embraces a multitude of possibilities, from animal, bird, fish or human forms, to minute organisms that can only be seen under a microscope. Leaf and flower forms, textures on tree bark, microscope views of plant cell structure can all inspire designs of great beauty and subtlety. However, execution of the design also plays a vital part in the success of the operation. How best to interpret your idea in metal? If you have undertaken experiments in technique, you will find that as you conceive a form, you will envisage the technique at almost the same time. Should you etch the form, interpret it with wires, laminate it with sheet metal, chase it, or punch a pattern? You may even decide to build up an interesting depth and variety by combining etching or piercing with applied wires or sheet. The choice is yours, but think hard about it and take a little time over it because it is important to get it right.

There are people who do not care for natural form as a basis for designing and prefer to use man-made objects as sources of reference. The forms may be found in everyday domestic surroundings, in electronics, in heavy engineering or in architecture. Anything that fascinates or intrigues you may well form the basis for a design. For instance, printed circuits for the electronics industry are often most attractive, or maps or photographs of cities can be quite intriguing. The methods of practical interpretation provide problems similar to those already discussed in relation to natural form, and the solutions can be found by experimenting and by trial runs with the techniques that have already been outlined.

The beginner, however, may appreciate that all the imagery that I have touched upon exists, but may not be able to tap any of it because of a lack of self-confidence or because of a lack of freehand drawing ability. He or she may, however, have quite exacting standards about the general, practical quality that silver or jewelry should have. This is the frustrating position in which older students often find themselves. Starting from realism is an obvious solution in the areas of decoration and jewelry, or the student may build three-dimensional patterns with wire and scrap metal, pushing them into a flat sheet of Plasticine. In the case of holloware, or abstract shapes in jewelry, proportions and shapes may be arrived at by using mathematical calculations of a simple nature. Logical variations of squares, circles and triangles can form the basis of pleasing shapes. Circles can be developed into ellipses, or oval shapes whose widths are two thirds of their length, or one third of the length. Proportions based upon one third divisions are often satisfying.

When you have drawn your design at least you can see something and proceed to alter it if you don't like it. So often it is the problem of visualizing in the first place any shape at all that prevents people from setting down an idea. Calculated methods like the ones just described may be of great help to you at first but once you have gained the confidence to put something down and have developed some form of judgement you should drop the methods because they will tend to rule you and prevent your judgement from developing further. Similarly, although drawing instruments like compasses and rulers may help you when you first start designing, they are a positive bar to producing subtle forms, and the sooner you undergo the painful experience of learning to control your pencil or pen the better.

Another method of approaching design is through the materials themselves. To take a piece of metal and to hammer it and watch it change shape or section, or to bend it and observe the quality of curve that results, is to dabble with aesthetics and form in a practical manner. It is a slow method, and undoubtedly what you learn has to be pulled together by drawing, but once again it may be your way into the world of designing. Aluminium sheet can be most useful if you are employing this method, or even paper or cardboard joined with Sellotape may help you to envisage the idea more clearly. In point of fact these methods can be used during various stages of drawn designing, and they are sometimes very helpful when difficult shapes have to be calculated before cutting out the metal.

Another approach to design is that which considers the function of the object first. You may find, if you do this, that many problems are solved for you even before you put pencil to paper. The subtle curve on a handle may make it impossible to hold, or the intriguing decoration on the side of a tankard may prove a haven for microbes and a distinct health hazard! The decoration around a finger ring may make the ring too thick or rough and the curve that you think will look good on a collar or necklace may well prevent it from sitting properly around the neck and on the shoulders. A drinking vessel which is the wrong diameter can cause awkward problems if your nose gets in the way as you are drinking, and one that has very flared and sloping sides is difficult to carry or lift without spilling the liquid. If you design cutlery and handles to fit the hand comfortably, and to be positioned at the right angle, they are likely to look good. If you design them as awkward shapes, and in thin, sharp materials, they will look weak and uncomfortable, and will be weak and uncomfortable to hold and use. You can often turn an apparent problem to your advantage. Hinges on boxes or pots and necklace links need not be disguised in a tortuous and complicated manner, but may be honestly used to become a feature and even a decorative element of the design. In a similar manner catches and fastenings on jewelry may be designed to be seen and accepted as part of the visual appeal of the object.

Ideally, you should consider all the approaches at the same time – and the experienced designer does learn to do this – but I would emphasize again that it is not possible for the beginner. So work from your strengths, realize your weaknesses and try to improve gradually. A design note and sketch book is invaluable so that you can constantly record information and ideas and develop designs. Never be satisfied with one solution to a problem, always attempt to produce at least three ideas, and having produced them, develop them before you rush to produce them in three dimensions. Obviously, you must set a time limit on your designing time, but don't stop too early because you never know what is around the corner.

Conversion Factors

Weight

To convert:

Ounces troy to grammes	multiply by		31·1034768
Grammes to ounces troy	,,	,,	0·0321507466
Ounces avoirdupois to grammes	,,	,,	28·3495
Grammes to ounces avoirdupois	,,	,,	0·035274
Kilograms to ounces troy	,,	,,	32·1507

Length

To convert:

Millimetres to inches	multiply by		0·0393701
Inches to millimetres	,,	,,	25·4
Metres to inches	,,	,,	39·3701
Inches to metres	,,	,,	0·0254
Feet to metres	,,	,,	0·3048
Metres to feet	,,	,,	3·28084

Area and volume

To convert:

Square inches to square millimetres	multiply by		645·16
Square millimetres to square inches	,,	,,	0·00155
Cubic inches to cubic centimetres	,,	,,	16·3871
Cubic centimetres to cubic inches	,,	,,	0·0610237

Rounded metric conversions

The following are simple, *approximate* conversions:

1 ounce Troy	=	30 grammes
1 inch	=	25 millimetres
4 inches	=	101 millimetres
1 foot	=	300 millimetres

Troy Weight

24 grains = 1 penny weight
20 penny weights = 1 ounce
12 ounces = 1 pound

British Association Threads
Tables for drilling holes
and metric dimensions

B.A. number	0	1	2	3	4	5	6	7	8	9	10
Diameter of tap in mm	6·0	5·3	4·7	4·1	3·6	3·2	2·8	2·6	2·2	1·9	1·7
Size of drill for tap (number)	10	17	24	29	32	37	43	46	50	52	54
Clearance drill in mm	6·1	5·4	4·8	4·2	3·7	3·3	2·9	2·6	2·25	1·95	1·75

Useful gauge comparisons

Thicknesses in decimal inches and millimetres.
Weight of standard (0.925) silver per square inch or
per square centimetre for most gauges.

Thickness (mm) (ins)	B.M.G. (Birmingham metal gauge)	S.W.G. (Standard wire gauge)	Browne & Sharpe	United States Standard	Standard 0·925 weight per sq. in. (oz)	Silver weight per sq. cm (g)
0·406 0·016	6	—	—	—	0·090	0·41
0·417 0·016	—	27	—	—	—	—
0·432 0·017	—	—	—	27	—	—
0·455 0·018	—	—	25	—	0·098	—
0·457 0·018	—	26	—	26	—	—
0·483 0·019	7	—	—	—	0·107	0·52
0·508 0·020	—	25	—	—	—	—
0·511 0·020	—	—	24	—	0·110	—
0·546 0·021	8	—	—	—	0·121	0·57
0·550 0·021	—	—	—	25	—	—
0·559 0·022	—	24	—	—	—	—
0·574 0·023	—	—	23	—	0·123	—
0·610 0·024	9	23	—	—	0·136	0·62
0·635 0·025	—	—	—	24	—	—
0·643 0·025	—	—	22	—	0·138	—
0·711 0·028	10	22	—	23	0·155	0·72
0·724 0·028	—	—	21	—	0·158	—
0·790 0·031	—	—	—	22	—	—
0·801 0·032	—	—	20	—	0·174	—
0·813 0·032	11	21	—	—	0·181	0·82
0·863 0·034	—	—	—	21	—	—
0·889 0·035	12	—	—	—	0·196	0·93
0·912 0·035	—	—	19	—	0·198	—
0·914 0·036	—	20	—	—	—	—
0·930 0·037	—	—	—	20	—	—
0·965 0·038	13	—	—	—	0·215	0·99
1·016 0·040	—	19	—	—	—	—
1·024 0·040	—	—	18	—	0·220	—
1·092 0·043	14	—	—	19	0·243	1·13
1·151 0·045	—	—	17	—	0·247	—
1·219 0·048	15	18	—	—	0·272	1·23
1·290 0·050	—	—	16	—	0·277	—
1·295 0·051	16	—	—	—	0·289	1·33

Thickness		B.M.G. (Birmingham metal gauge)	S.W.G. (Standard wire gauge)	Browne & Sharpe	United States Standard	Standard 0·925 weight per sq. in.	Silver weight per sq. cm
(mm)	(ins)					(oz)	(g)
1·350	0·053	—	—	—	18	—	—
1·397	0·055	17	—	—	—	0·300	—
1·422	0·056	—	17	—	17	—	—
1·450	0·057	—	—	15	—	0·311	—
1·499	0·059	18	—	—	—	0·344	—
1·575	0·062	19	—	—	16	0·350	—
1·626	0·064	—	16	—	—	—	—
1·629	0·065	—	—	14	—	0·351	—
1·651	0·065	20	—	—	—	—	1·70

Approximate weights of standard (0.925) silver circles in Birmingham Metal Gauge,

with decimal inch and millimetre equivalents

Diam. of circle	B.M.G.	9	10	11	12	13	14	15	16	17	18
	ins	0·024	0·028	0·032	0·035	0·038	0·043	0·048	0·051	0·055	0·0
	mm	0·610	0·711	0·813	0·889	0·965	1·092	1·219	1·295	1·397	1·4
ins						oz					
4		1·71	2·00	2·28	2·50	2·71	3·07	3·42	3·64	3·92	4·
4½		2·16	2·53	2·89	3·16	3·43	3·88	4·33	4·60	4·96	5·
5		2·67	3·12	3·57	3·90	4·23	4·79	5·35	5·68	6·13	6·
5½		3·24	3·77	4·32	4·72	5·12	5·80	6·47	6·88	7·41	7·
6		3·85	4·49	5·14	5·62	6·10	6·90	7·70	8·18	8·82	9·
6½		4·52	5·27	6·03	6·59	7·16	8·10	9·04	9·60	10·35	11·
7		5·24	6·11	6·99	7·65	8·30	9·39	10·48	11·14	12·01	12·
7½		6·02	7·02	8·03	8·78	9·52	10·78	12·04	12·79	13·78	14·
8		6·84	7·99	9·13	9·99	10·84	12·26	13·69	14·55	15·68	16·
8½		7·73	9·01	10·31	11·27	12·23	13·84	15·44	16·43	17·70	18·
9		8·66	10·10	11·56	12·64	13·72	15·52	17·33	18·42	19·85	21·
9½		9·65	11·26	12·88	14·08	15·28	17·29	19·31	20·52	22·12	23·
10		10·69	12·48	14·28	15·60	16·92	19·16	21·40	22·74	24·50	26·
10½		11·79	13·76	15·73	17·20	18·67	21·12	23·59	25·07	27·02	28·
11		12·94	15·10	17·27	18·88	20·49	23·18	25·89	27·51	29·65	31·
11½		14·14	16·50	18·87	20·62	22·39	25·34	28·30	30·07	32·41	34·
12		15·40	17·97	20·55	22·47	24·38	27·59	30·81	32·74	35·29	37·

Approximate weights of square wire

inches (fractions)	inches (decimal)	mm	ounces per foot	grams per metre
1/16	0·062	1·588	0·25	26
3/32	0·093	1·984	0·60	61
1/8	0·125	3·175	1·00	102
3/16	0·187	4·763	2·20	225
1/4	0·250	6·350	4·00	408

Glossary

Anneal When metal has been marked, bent or hammered its grain structure is distorted causing tension in the metal and making it hard. This can be restored by annealing or heating the metal to the correct temperature.

Bench pin A piece of wood which projects from the work bench and has a V cut into it, so that two tapered prongs project towards the craftsman. It is invaluable for holding work while filing and sawing are carried out.

Bezel A collar of sheet metal which may form the wall of a setting for a cabochon stone, or may be the metal collar on a lid which fits into the body and keeps the lid in position. In rectangular boxes the bezel is usually in the box, and the lid fits onto and over it.

Borax Commonly used by silversmiths and jewellers as a flux where solder is to be applied to a joint. Borax may be obtained in two forms: as powder that should be mixed with water and painted onto the joint area, and as a hard cone which should be held in one hand and, with a circular movement, ground with a little water onto an unglazed stoneware dish or a piece of slate until a thick paste results. This, too, should be painted onto the joint area of the work.

Burnish To polish metal by rubbing it with a highly polished agate or steel tool, often long and oval in section, using a soap solution as a lubricant.

Caulk To thicken the edge of a raised form as raising proceeds, by striking it with a hammer.

Cabochon Stone whose underside is flat, but whose plan may be circular, rectangular, or triangular, and whose upper surfaces form a dome. The dome may be shallow, deep, pointed, or constant in the curve of its profile.

Chamfer The angle which is cut on each of two plates which are to be joined to form an L shape, like the corner of a box. To make a right angle, each edge of the metal must be filed to an angle of 45°. U.S.: Mitering or beveling.

Clinker   Carborundum grains or lump pumice (U.S.).

Collet hammer   Planishing hammer with a face curved slightly in only one direction (U.S.).

Cotter pins   Sometimes called split pins, they are pieces of half-round wire bent double and usually used to prevent nuts becoming unscrewed from spindles, or to prevent wheels from coming off axles. In silversmithing they are usually used to hold wires tight up to sheet during soldering operations.

Cowls   Dust collecting hood, used in polishing (U.S.).

Cuttlefish casting An elementary method of casting employing cuttle-bone, and called cuttlebone casting in U.S.

Doming block   Brass or steel cube with several semicircular hollows of different sizes distributed around the faces. Sheet metal is punched into these hollows. It is an invaluable piece of equipment for a jeweller. U.S.: Dapping die.

Draw-plate   Steel plate in which two or three rows of tapered holes have been pierced. The holes are graded in size, and wire can be pulled through each hole in turn, starting with the largest, so that it is gradually reduced in diameter. Draw-plates can be obtained with round, square, oval, triangular, rectangular, half-round and knife-edge holes.

Enameling silver   In the U.S. fine silver (999 parts pure silver) is used. It has a melting point of 960.5°C (1760.9°F) and a specific gravity of 10.5.

Escapement file   Extremely fine cut needle file or jeweler's file (U.S.).

Etchant   Mordant (U.S.).

Flare (Fault)   If too much metal is raised in at the bottom of a tall form, the sides take on a concave or flared elevation. The body must be raised from the point at which the flare becomes evident if the metal is not to be seriously thinned and probably cracked.

Flash   Metal that has run into a crack in the mould of a casting and shows itself as a ragged sheet or fin projecting from the completed casting.

Hearth   Soldering pan (U.S.).

Holloware   Term used to describe vessels that are hollow such as bowls, coffee pots, and jugs.

Horse Tool for holding stakes so that a piece of deep holloware can be planished or raised well down the sides or near the bottom. It is made from square-section steel and has a hole at each end, into which a stake may be fitted. One end is always cranked to allow work on a difficult shape. A horse may have a stem welded to its centre section so that it can be set into a bench or a tree trunk, or alternatively it can be fastened in a vice.

Horse's head stakes Mushroom stakes (U.S.).

Linisher Machine with a moving emery-cloth belt tensioned between two rollers, one of which is driven by an electric motor. The belt passes, grit uppermost, over a metal plate, and work can be applied to the belt at this point to cut away its surface. U.S.: Band-sander.

Mandrel See Triblet.

Mops Buffs made of muslin, flannel, cotton, or wool and secured with stitching or leather (U.S.).

Paillons Small pieces of solder, sometimes called panels.

Pantagraph A mechanical engraving machine, which can also be used to undertake miniature milling operations. It is an expensive machine suitable for colleges or commercial workshops.

Pickle Any acid solution or proprietary acid substitute which is used to clean metal after annealing or to remove borax after soldering. Such a solution is usually kept in deep, lead-lined tanks which may or may not be heated.

Piercing saw Jeweler's saw (U.S.).

Planish To smooth metal, an operation always carried out with a planishing hammer by a silversmith.

Raise To produce a deep vessel from thin metal by hammering it over a metal stake.

Riffler File with curved ends which may be circular, oval, triangular, or rectangular in section. Only the ends have cutting surfaces, the centre being smooth for comfortable holding. Rifflers will reach into awkward places that are beyond ordinary files.

Scribe To score a line in the surface of metal with a pointed steel rod.

Sink To produce shallow dishes and bowls by hammering thick metal systematically to stretch all but a strip around the outer edge. The original diameter of the metal remains unaltered and the stretched metal becomes the depth.

Sprue Wax wire attached to a wax model to be embedded in investment plaster for lost wax casting. There may be several sprues on a model. When all the wax has been melted out of an embedded model, it is down the sprue holes that the molten metal will enter the mould.

Standard silver In the U.S. this is called sterling silver, an alloy of 925 parts silver to 75 parts copper, which has a melting point of 893°C (1640°F) and a specific gravity of 10.4–10.6.

Swage block Steel block with a graded series of semicircular channels running across it. Strip metal, when hammered into a swage block, curves around to form the basis of a metal tube.

Triblet A straight, tapered steel stake upon which rings and settings can be shaped, enlarged, and hammered. A triblet is usually circular in section, but triblets with oval, square, or triangular sections are useful tools to possess. Ring triblets usually have a machine-textured, cylindrical handle at the wider end. The handle can be clamped in a vice during working operations so that the craftsman's hands are left free to hold work and a hammer or a mallet. Large triblets stand upright on the bench, point uppermost, and are often called bench mandrels.

Tripoli Fine, abrasive grit which is usually bonded with tallow and moulded into a long narrow bar. Sold as tripoli compound it is used in the first stages of machine polishing, or with a leather stick for hand polishing.

Water of Ayr stone Grey slate sold in square sticks of varying sizes and used to grind the surface of metal (with water as a lubricant) to remove scratches and other blemishes. U.S.: Carborundum sticks, sometimes called Scotch stone.

List of Suppliers

Great Britain

Silver and gold, sheet, wire and tube, and jewellers' findings, solders and fluxes

J. Blundell and Sons Ltd,
(not fluxes)
199 Wardour Street,
London W1.

Johnson Matthey Metals Ltd,
81 Hatton Garden,
London EC1.

Vittoria Street,
Birmingham 1.

175 Arundel Gate,
Sheffield 1.

Sheffield Smelting Company,
134–136 St John Street,
London EC1.

Warstone Lane,
Birmingham 18.

Royds Mills,
Windsor Street,
Sheffield 4.

Copper, gilding metal, nickel and stainless steel sheet, strip wire and tube

H. Righton & Co. Ltd,
Brook Vale Road,
Witton,
Birmingham 6.

70 Pentonville Road,
London N1.

Hand tools, polishers, abrasives, findings, jewelry boxes etc.

H. S. Walsh & Sons Ltd,
Beckenham,
Kent.

E. C. Gray — H. S. Walsh,
12 Clerkenwell Road,
London EC1.

Charles Cooper,
12 Hatton Wall,
London EC1.

F. Pike,
58G Hatton Garden,
London EC1.

C. V. Salvo Ltd,
88 Hatton Garden,
London EC1.

T. Sutton Ltd,
Frederick Street,
Birmingham 1.

Stakes, mandrels, hearths, turntables etc.

F. R. Willmore,
210 Leicester Road,
Loughborough,
Leicestershire.

Polishing materials, electro-plating equipment etc.

W. Canning & Co. Ltd,
Great Hampton Street,
Birmingham 18.

Casting equipment, materials and manuals

Hoben Davis Ltd,
Spencroft Road,
Holditch Industrial Estate,
Newcastle-Under-Lyme,
Staffs.

W. J. Hooker Ltd,
Waterside,
Brightlingsea,
Essex.

Engineers' tools, lathes etc.

Buck & Hickman Ltd,
P.O. Box No. 33,
23–32 Whittal Street,
Birmingham 4.

Buck & Ryan,
101 Tottenham Court Road,
London W1.

Enamels

W. G. Ball Ltd,
Longton Mill,
Anchor Road,
Longton,
Stoke-on-Trent,
Staffs.

Enamels

Crafts Unlimited
(Schauer Enamels)
21 Macklin Street,
London WC2.

Wengers Ltd,
Etruria,
Stoke-on-Trent,
Staffs.

Sculptors' supplies, polyester resin and pigments

Personal shoppers only:
Alec Tiranti Ltd,
21 George Place,
London W1.

Mail order:
70 High Street,
Theale,
Berks.

Technical information
Technical Advisory Committee
Worshipful Company of Goldsmiths

Central House,
Whitechapel High Street,
London E1.

British Assay Offices

Goldsmiths Hall, Gutter Lane, London EC2.

Newhall Street, Birmingham

Portobello Street, Sheffield 1.

15 Queen Street, Edinburgh 2.

United States

Findings, solders, and fluxes

ALLCRAFT TOOL AND SUPPLY
COMPANY
22 West 48th Street,
New York,
N.Y. 10036 (N.Y. Salesroom)

204 North Harbor Blvd.,
Fullerton,
Calif. 92632 (Calif. salesroom)

215 Park Avenue,
Hicksville,
N.Y. 11801 (Mail orders)

Anchor Alloys, Inc.
966 Meeker Avenue,
Brooklyn,
N.Y.

Anchor Tool and Supply
Company
231 Main Street,
Chatham,
N.J. 07928

GENERAL FINDINGS
7049½ Vineland Avenue,
N. Hollywood,
Calif. 91605

608 Fifth Avenue,
New York,
N.Y. 10020

801 East Marion Street,
Arlington Heights,
Chicago,
Ill. 60004

Kester Solder Company
88 Ferguson Street,
Newark, N.J.

Precious Metals

American Metal Climax, Inc.
1270 Avenue of the Americas,
New York

T.B. Hagstoz and Son
709 Sansom Street,
Philadelphia,
Pa. 19106

HANDY AND HARMAN
850 Third Avenue,
New York,
N.Y. 10022

4140 Gibson Road,
El Monte,
Calif. 91731

1900 Estes Avenue,
Elk Grove Village,
Illinois 60007

Frank Mossberg Drive,
Attleboro,
Mass., 02703

4402 West 215th Street
Cleveland,
Ohio 44126

17000 West 8 Mile Road,
Southfield,
Michigan 48075

1234 Exchange Bank Bldg.,
Dallas,
Texas 75235

C.R. Hill Company
2734 West 11 Mile Road,
Berkley,
Mich. 48072

Hoover and Strong
119 Tupper Street,
Buffalo,
N.Y. 14201

Leach and Garner Company
608 Fifth Avenue,
New York

Copper and other metals

T.E. Conklin Brass and
Copper Company, Inc.
324 West 23rd Street,
New York,
N.Y. 10011

Horton-Angell Company
Attleboro,
Massachusetts

Revere Copper and Brass, Inc.
230 Park Avenue,
New York,
N.Y. 10010

White Metal Rolling and
Stamping Corp.
80 Moultrie Street,
Brooklyn, N.Y.

Technical Information

Superintendent of Documents
United States General Printing
Office Washington, D.C.

*General tools, including handtools,
polishers, abrasives, files, etc.*

Allcraft Tool and Supply
Company (see above)

Anchor Tool and Supply
Company (see above)

Brodhead Garrett and Company
4560 East 71st Street,
Cleveland, Ohio

Craftool, Inc.
396 Broadway, New York 10013

William Dixon Company
Carlstadt,
New Jersey 07072

Friedheim Tool Supply Company
412 West 6th Street,
Los Angeles,
Calif. 90014

I. Schor, Inc.
71 Fifth Avenue,
New York,
N.Y. 10003

Imperial Buff Company
236 Stagg Street,
Brooklyn, N.Y.

The LEA Manufacturing
Company
237 East Aurora Street,
Waterbury,
Conn. 06720

Nicholson File Company
Providence, R.I.

Assay Information

United States Government
National Bureau of Standards
Washington, D.C.

Poly-Products Corporation
Monrovia, California

SWEST, INC.
10803 Composite Drive,
Dallas,
Texas 75220

118 Broadway,
San Antonio,
Texas 78295

1725 Victory Blvd.,
Glendale,
Calif. 91201

*Casting equipment and sculptors'
supplies*

Casting Supply House
62 West 47 Street,
New York

Centrifugal Casting Supply
Company
17 West 60 Street,
New York

Sculpture House
38 East 30 Street,
New York,
N.Y. 10016

Enamels

Allcraft Tool and Supply
Company (see above)

Thomas C. Thompson
1539 Deerfield Road,
Highland Park,
Ill.

Bibliography

Charron, Shirley, *Modern Pewter*, Van Nostrand Reinhold, New York, 1973

Choate, Sharr, *Creative Casting*, Allen & Unwin, London, and Crown, New York, 1966

Choate, Sharr, *Creative Gold and Silversmithing*, Crown, New York, 1970

Cuzner, Bernard, *A Silversmith's Manual*, N.A.G. Press, London

Franke, Lois E., *Handwrought Jewelry*, McKnight and McKnight, Bloomington, Ill., 1962

Hughes, Graham, *The Art of Jewelry*, Studio Vista, London, and Viking, New York, 1972

Hughes, Graham, *Modern Silver Throughout the World*, Studio Vista, London, 1967

Maryon, Herbert, *Metalwork and Enamelling*, Chapman and Hall, London, and Dover, New York, 1959 (4th edition)

Newble, Brian, *Practical Enamelling and Jewelry Work*, Studio Vista, London, and Viking, New York, 1967

Seeler, Margaret, *The Art of Enamelling*, Van Nostrand Reinhold, New York, 1969

Thomas, Richard, *Metalsmithing for the Artist Craftsman*, Chilton, Radnor, Pa., 1960

Untracht, Oppi, *Metal Techniques for Craftsmen*, Hale, London, 1969, and Doubleday, New York, 1968

Von Neumann, Robert, *The Design and Creation of Jewelry*, Chilton, Radnor, Pa., 1967

Wilson, Harry, *Silver Work and Jewelry*, Pitman, London, 1948

Index

Figures in italics refer to illustrations